Dedicated to my mother, Ida Montehermoso,
and in loving memory of my father, Edgar Strova.

THE SECRET LANGUAGE
OF BELLY DANCING

Euclid Public Library
631 East 222nd Street
Euclid, OH 44123
(216) 261-5300

MARIA STROVA

The Secret Language of

Belly Dancing

Symbols

Sensuality

Maternity

Forgotten Roots

MACRO
EDIZIONI

DISCLAIMER

Note: This book has been translated from Italian to English. The bibliography contains the Italian information for most research materials. Due to time constraints and unavailable sources, some English texts may vary from the original version; however, all references have been cited with the author's name. The editor can be contacted for any unidentified material. Many thanks to those who supplied photos and information.

translation	Kathryn Kelley
editing	Valentina Pieri e Matteo Venturi
cover	Matteo Venturi

Ist edition October 2005

Collana "Biblioteca del Benessere", a cura di Valerio Pignatta

© 2005 **Macro Edizioni**
www.macroedizioni.it
Via Savona 66
47023 Diegaro di Cesena (FC)
ISBN 88-7507-616-2

Contents

Acknowledgements

First and foremost I would like to thank my beloved Calogero, who eagerly supported my research and, with dedication, worked hard to make one of our dreams come true: The Omphalos Theater. Thanks to my daughter Martinica for the spontaneous dances she dedicates to me and for her poetry which has always inspired me and filled me with pride. Thanks to my sons, Leandro and Gabriel, who teach me to see the world through their eyes and shower me with kisses. And to Federica, I hope we'll dance together someday. I would like to recognize all my family and friends who have been with me along the way, in particular, Francesca, and my niece, Anita, who has been one of my youngest and most talented students.

I would like to thank all of my dance teachers over the years: Akopov, who taught me as a young girl to go above and beyond the technique. To my belly dancing instructors, Ahmed Hussein, Yousry Sharif, and Elena Lentini from New York, infinite thanks for your generosity and for teaching me so many secrets of the dance. To Ibrahim Farrah, who has tragically disappeared: I have fond memories of your superb choreography and your passion for the dance. To Laurie Rose, Mesmera from Los Angeles, thank you for helping me cultivate a world of feminine images that were unknown to me at the time. To Mohamed Kordanian, for teaching me the delicacy of the Persian dance, and for his extreme dedication to the art, which even being imprisoned in Iran couldn't stop. To Sarah, Mahmood, Rheda, Raqia Hassan from Cairo, infinite thanks for the refinement and musical quality they passed on to me through their styles. To Delilah in Seattle and to my friend and obstetrician, Ornella Fantini, for having helped me discover dancing during pregnancy.
I would like to recognize the instructors Peter Flood, Lilly Parker, and the actress Ellen Burstyn of the Actors' Studio New York, because my dance has been truly enriched by the art of acting which I learned with them.

In Italy, I would like to thank Saad Ismail and Esmat Osman, who has sadly disappeared, for making me feel at home when I first came to Rome and for having given me the invite to dance at the Academy of Egypt, a night that changed my life and that I will always remember fondly.
To Julia Mion at the Qamar Association in Udine, a heartfelt shimmy for her enthusiasm about my work and for inspiring me to take more risks.
A thought of gratitude for all of my fellow teachers who keep this art alive and have the mutual interest of improving.
Infinite thanks to my classical yoga instructor, Piero Verri, because it was at the end of the fifth year of his Brahmananda instructor training course in Rome that I really felt the need to write this book, without being too afraid to do it.

To Justyna Suska, an affectionate *dziekuje*, because without her kind cooperation at home, I wouldn't have been able to dedicate all the necessary hours to dance and write at the same time.

A very special thanks to the artist Ettore de Conciliis, for having believed in my work from the beginning, for the beneficial dinners with friends, and for the inspiration I take from his sensual paintings of primordial nature. Thanks to Janice Kyd for her generous spirit and her suggestions on the text; to Filippo Bettini for his encouragement and initial reading of the book, to Kathryn Kelley for translating the book from Italian into English. To Simonetta Retica and Alessandro Casini for their time and effort spent on the graphic design. To Jimmy Webb, I'm, very grateful not only for his example as a musical poet and author, but also for his attentive and affectionate emails that gave me guidance all the way from New York.

Finally, I'd like to thank from the bottom of my heart, the many women who have taken or are taking lessons and have participated in my seminars. Their dances and opinions contributed to making this book happen. They are my collective muse. To all of those who have written to me, expressing their appreciation of my work, thank you again, because your words helped me get through many moments of doubt.

Foreword

This book, *The Secret Language of Belly Dancing*, has among its many merits, the privilege of explaining that today an evolution of this ancient dance is taking place. There are changes being made to the Eastern stereotypes in the touristic and commercial forms that we are used to. It is a cultural evolution that is allowing the art of belly dancing to become more appreciated and widespread, by now in all corners of the world, without being restricted by borders.

Through her words, Maria Strova shares the story of her life and experience as a dancer. At the same time, she offers interesting reflections, historical research, and photographs relating to dance and in particular, belly dancing.

Maria leaves her homeland of Colombia at the young age of seventeen, following her instinct and the constant flow of emigration from the Latin American countries to North America. One day, as she tells us, while walking along a New York street, she hears a sound, the rhythm of a drum.

This is an important event for her, that must have shaken her in the depths of her soul, and that reveals her future as a dancer. From that moment, she carries this sound with her: when she studies dance in New York, when she works as an actress in Los Angeles' world of cinema, when she travels towards the Orient, the Mediterranean, and finally to Rome to get married, have children, dance, teach, manage a theater/school and write these pages.

Hers is a fascinating journey through diverse cultures. A journey not only through space, but also through time, as you will see in this literary work. The author explores the mysteries of mythology to find the origins and the meaning of dance, which for her, is art and poetry. Her roots can be found in a primordial past, in the wisdom of the Great Mother and of Mother Earth, in nature and in her signs.

Maria Strova includes a great deal of bibliographical research; she provides a wide variety of informative facts, as well as her personal advice for those who want to dance….. This is her way of revealing to herself and others her own experience and the meaning of her vital position at the center of her dance. As a whole, the book is a message naturally geared towards women, but it seems to me that the power of its contents could really be of interest to any reader.

All in all, these pages aid us in exploring and redefining in modern terms the ancient language of belly dancing and the beauty of the life that it celebrates. In this way, the femininity and sensuality of women, the veil that the dancer moves through space, the music and the costumes…all of these things become renewed together.

Like the waves of the sea that eternally repeat themselves, always taking different forms, the movements of this dance repeat themselves in a new way, again and again, through the eternity of time.

And so, the book lies in front of you…..

Ettore de Conciliis

My Secret Dance

*N*ew York, the city where East meets West, it was there that I disco-vered belly dancing and "The East" that lived inside of me, wi-thout a fight, but instead with love, I let myself be seduced by its language of peace.

Looking in the dictionary at the various synonyms for secret, I see: intimacy, in-timate, deep, mystery, arcane, enigma, bond, deceit, hidden, latent, concealed, innermost, reserved, private, occult, clandestine, discreet; but also method, mo-de, recipe, device, all the way until illegal, subterranean.

In my life, these words have come to life as synonyms for dance, to which I de-dicate myself: the art of belly dancing. I grew up in Colombia, submerged in the feminine universe of my five elderly and wonderful aunts, who told us stories about the past while my parents were at work. I listened in amazement along with my sisters Idita and Alexandra. From a young age, we learned to make up our own games and create from what we had around us. The dance shows that we put on for our aunts and our family gave me my first lesson in the art of im-provisation: to be able to express at that very moment the workings of the soul. Along with our dance performances, we were also fond of hiding shoes in pil-lows...a surprise for whoever stretched out on the bed, putting his or her head back on the pillow, and getting a good little bang instead. As for bangs on the head, I got my share, but now I am grateful for them because this game, as com-monplace as it may seem, taught me to take a second look at things and to search for things that may be hidden.

Among the three of us, there was a sense of understanding, and a love that was since-re, which has remained intact over the years and through the struggles. Our parents didn't raise us with the rules often reserved for daughters ("you can't go out alone," "that's not for girls," or "think about getting married"). On the contrary, they encou-raged us to make choices that today I consider quite bold, for example, travelling abroad at a young age...something that has allowed each of us to follow our destinies. At nine years old, I secretly dreamed about classical dance, about the tutu and the mysterious glide of ballerinas on their tip toes. It made me sigh and feel a painful longing at the same time. I saw myself on stage, but I couldn't bring myself to ask my parents for lessons, because I was afraid they would tell me that we couldn't afford them. So I continued to dance in my own imagination and, in secret, I called the dance schools that I found listed in the phone book to ask, in a hushed voice, when the courses began, and the dreaded question, how much they cost. One day I told my parents of my sufferings and, having picked up on my artistic ability, they took me to the state school of dance for a try out; I passed it and began to study classical dance.

So I continued to dance in my own imagination and, in secret, I called the dance schools...

As a teenager, when I started to go out with boys, dance became my secret measure, an imperceptible compatibility test that revealed the soul of my suitor without any cunning. Before getting to the conversation, we would dance a salsa or cumbia, something with a rhythm that conjures up the heartbeat of a person in love.

Psychology and sensual expression have always been linked to the body for me, to the inherent rhythm of dance...

Psychology and sensual expression have always been linked to the body for me, to the inherent rhythm of dance, and to the language of our gestures. It is a part of my Latin culture and something that I trust in situations that seem most hopeless. Like when I have to vote and make a choice between two political candidates; instead of listening to their arguments on TV, I turn off the volume and watch their gestures, their "dance," and based on the information that I gather from their body language, I make my decision. I know that while their words are aimed, above all, at convincing us to believe what they are saying, the body rarely lies. Of course after that we can only wait and see....

Thanks to my passion for the truth, which I found in my body and in dance, at the end of high school I was spared a bad grade in Chemistry that would have yanked me right out of my dreams of traveling. I had heard about New York, the "Big Apple," the world center of dance, and I had secretly begun writing to the best schools of modern dance: Martha Graham, Alvin Ailey, Nikolais, Cunningham, all of which sent me back valuable brochures full of dance photos that made me go crazy with excitement and long to travel.

Consuelo, my friend from dance and later my travel buddy on our misadventures in America, shared this dream of going to New York with me. We went around like members of a secret society in a Russian school of dance, while we got ourselves ready for departure.

One of my very first dance performances in the opera, La Vedova Allegra (on the left, standing up). Teatro Colon in Bogota, Colombia.

Even today, in our telegraphic emails, we inevitably find ourselves talking about the hard times we went through, but we laugh about it, because both of us have overcome our obstacles and found the right path. It's a known fact that getting a visa to live in the U.S. is an impossible dream for many people in the "third world." In Colombia, you could pay up to $4000 to get one on the black market. Fortunately, we didn't have to resort to that. I finally got my hands on a visa after countless appointments at the embassy, and I celebrated with great joy.

It turned out that the biggest problem wasn't the visa, nor the fact that I was a minor, because my parents could sign for me at the airport and allow me to leave. It dealt with one little word that Consuelo and I found in all the brochures. We tried to translate it, but no dictionary could give us a definition that we liked: "tuition;" it seemed to me that it would have been more appropriate to translate it as "forbidden," than "cost of education."

I had learned from my parents that "las mujeres son unas verracas" (women have brains) and that "lo mas importante es que estudien" (the most important thing is to study), and with these ideas I decided to make the journey to New York and not to let whatever difficulties I would face get the best of me.

With my parents, I solved the problem of "tuition" by stretching my translation a little. I told them that the prices for the lessons were monthly and not daily, because I knew it was the most they could offer me. They accepted, trying to do everything possible to help me, but without making impossible promises. They couldn't think in Colombian pesos about something that needed to be thought about in dollars.

The tuition became my little secret and I thought that once I got to New York, I would be able to get down to business and find away out of this problem.

The impact of a city that is, essentially, hostile, and the need to adapt to the American mentality, the winter, and the English language, were all some of the things that I had failed to consider when I first dreamed about going there. They left a mark on me, but at the time, I didn't pay any attention to my feelings because my number one priority was finding a job without being able to speak English.

It's a law of economy that foreign workers are cheaper and take the most humbling jobs, usually the ones that the people from that area don't want to take. This may have been an unjust circumstance, but combined with my willingness, it allowed me to find work easily.

I started off selling Italian pastries, but then ended up eating too many of them. After leaving my adored *sfogliatelle* sweets, I went on to various different jobs, which taught me to be flexible and learn quickly. To keep one job, I learned how to mix a drink, make cappuccinos, and keep track of the bills in two days, and I did all of this while trying to avoid the wandering hands of my drunk manager, who always gave me a hard time about my age (I was only 18) and my English. I changed jobs frequently. I cleaned apartments and worked as a cashier in a few stores, but the money wasn't very good. I understood why the New York artists preferred to work as waiters and waitresses, because the hours were flexible and the pay was a lot better, but I got too tired doing that type of work, and after spending hours on my feet, it was too hard to go to dance lessons.

...an impossible dream for many people in the "third world"

"women have brains"

Dressed as a guerrilla on the set of Undercover in Los Angeles.

One day, I found a more relaxing job as a model and I started posing nude for a painter. Lying down with an apple in my hand, I made a tired Eve and often ended up falling asleep.

The painter liked it because the apple remained intact and her sleeping Eve seemed to have wanted to leave the question of the serpent for another day, so this element added tension to her painting.

I worked as a babysitter a few times, which I enjoyed because I was either in a family environment, or working in a big bookstore, where I had the opportunity to read and keep up one of my favorite pastimes that my father had instilled in us.

I also worked at a club until five in the morning and then had to take the train back to Brooklyn. The trip home on an almost empty train, with colorful characters giving me threatening looks, was the hardest part about the job. It taught me to be street wise, a self-defensive instinct that I had started to develop back in Colombia, where violence doesn't make first page news anymore.

Finally, I found a job that didn't tire me out too much before dance class. I worked as a hostess in Japanese piano bars, where you are required to stay seated and you make as much as you would waitressing in a restaurant.

Few people know these places where the businessmen go to relax or seal a deal, wining and dining their clients over the course of the evening. They buy good whiskey, which comes by the bottle and is served by the hostess. She then sits with the men to chat for a bit and lights their cigarettes. However, the smoke really got to me and was the thing that I hated most about the place. For this reason, I was slow to light my customers' cigarettes and "Mamma San," the owner of the bar, shot me looks of disapproval.

Being a foreigner, I knew I could act a little less servile than my Asian co-workers, and I had fun telling made-up stories about my day to keep me awake and to keep my personal life private. I never belly danced in these places; it would have been too provocative and would have gotten me in trouble. I limited myself to telling stories about my life and singing songs for the clients. I had perfect Japanese pronunciation, which made up for the fact that I was tone-deaf; it was easy for me because Japanese pronunciation is similar to that of Spanish.

When I went to dance the Argentine tango in Japan many years later- a job that I really loved- I sang one of my songs from the piano bar at the farewell dinner and the gesture was greatly appreciated.

The piano bar was the last side job I had before being able to support myself on acting and dancing alone. Only a very small percentage of artists (local and foreign alike) in the U.S. are able to live off their art without taking other jobs on the side.

They say that the United States (not to be confused with America since that includes all the countries of South, Central, and North America) is the land of opportunity, and I think it's true. You don't have opportunities based only on recommendations, but rather by overcoming obstacles and personal challenges and by paying your tuition.

The first opportunity that I was presented with was when the mythical innovator of modern dance, Martha Graham offered me a place at her school for Christmas. The word "tuition" had become familiar by then, so I did everything I could to afford this opportunity. I wanted to get to know up close the woman who had created a new type of dance with her unique vision.

Dancing with Michael Douglas at the Jewel of the Nile *premier in Regine's New York (photo used with permission of NY Post).*

One time, during a lesson, she asked me where I was from. This was a delicate subject for me, because I was afraid of being labeled and associated with Colombia's infamy for drugs and mafia.

People don't know much about my country of origin, and what they do know is usually negative, so I answered her hesitantly.

Martha Graham commanded great respect, and a little fear, because she got angry during lessons and rehearsals. But when she smiled, it was a realization for me, because I saw that she was surprised that a dancer coming from a "banana republic" could have a solid background and technique.

Her behavior gave me a stronger desire to participate in the cultural life of the city. I made a real effort to learn English, but like all immigrants, I was held back by the stamp on my visa, which was about to expire at that point.

In the euphoria of having obtained a visa in the first place, I hadn't bothered to inform myself of the few, but rigid restrictions I was subjected to: I couldn't leave the school that I had chosen and applied to from the brochures (which was like buying a CD because you like the cover…doesn't tell you much about the music), and I was required to leave the country after a year.

I could have gone home and forgotten about my dreams, or I could have refused to leave the country, joining the underground world of the many immigrants who stay without a visa: illegal aliens. I was 21 years old, and I chose option number two.

> **People don't know much about my country of origin, and what they do know is usually negative…**

> **I could have gone home and forgotten about my dreams, or I could have stayed illegally…**

Veil dance in Los Angeles

Trying to make up for the loneliness and anguish of my situation, I found comfort in eating and I put on a lot of weight. I lost my physical agility and I began to hate my body.

The more I suffered, the more I ate. I followed radical diets without much luck, and I swallowed pills that were supposed to make my hunger disappear. I finally resorted to bulimia to get some relief. I came to find out that in the world of dance, this is a common disease. When I used to go to the school bathrooms after lunch, they often smelled of vomit, and sometimes I heard the dancers exchanging advice on the "safest" ways to regurgitate food.

I worked double shifts as a waitress in nice restaurants, and at the end of the day, all I could do was go back to my hole on 1st and 12th in the East Village. Now, it wasn't a very chic area, actually it was quite dangerous, but I was happy because it was Manhattan. I went around with the tough attitude that I had acquired back in Cali when I was a young girl going to dance school alone. I didn't let anyone know that I was Latina, and I didn't speak Spanish with anyone because it was the language of drug dealers. One night the Immigration police came looking for me; I didn't understand why they had come for me, with all the drug dealersaround in the neighborhood, but they put me in the cruiser and took me to jail. They never tell you who called Immigration to give them your name. However, I am sure that for me it was a certain man who I had met in the past; he had an artificial leg, I remember. My roommate at the time had told me that this man could help me legalize my status to remain in the country, since he worked in Immigration. I trusted him because I was desperate, but I didn't know that he wanted sexual favors in return. After I refused him, he called Immigration.

The most embarrassing part of the experience wasn't the infamous mug shot that they take of criminals, with the lines on the wall behind you showing your height. At that moment I was too concentrated on not crying, fearing that they would have sent the photo to my parents. It wasn't even the fact that, in prison, I had to go to the bathroom with the door open since they counted us at various points throughout the day, even when we were in there…that just made me more indignant than anything else. What was most embarrassing for me was my trembling body and the noise of my chattering teeth in the back of the police car, and not being able to control myself. It got to the point where the others who were in trouble just like me, stared at me with curiosity while they took us away. I had never before experienced the same type of intense fear. I was barely able to control myself, but at the same time, I asked myself to be brave. In jail, you are always waiting for someone or something: a phone call, good news, an order, a lawyer; at least I think that's how it is as long as there's still the hope of getting out.

While I waited, I had dancing as my anchor. I found a space, and I gripped the bar of the bed to do my warm-up movements, which helped me keep it together and breathe. In this not-so-orthodox way I learned how to center myself and to use dance to express even the most overwhelming pain. This whole experience became a painful secret, and I never said anything to my parents because I wanted to keep them from suffering over something for which they could offer no immediate help.

…most embarrassing for me was my trembling body and the noise of my chattering teeth in the back of the police car, and not being able to control myself…

On a camel near the pyramids.

I was determined to make a future for myself and to find my way in New York...

I was determined to make a future for myself and to find my way in New York. And with little time left at my disposition before I was to be deported, I received help from the very few but very precious people who didn't abandon me. What happened after that will forever remain deep inside of me; I can only say that it was important in making me a mature woman, and in helping me find belly dancing, which came into my life after this period and gave me great comfort.

I was already a radiant and legal immigrant, walking the streets of NY and going around to the go-sees, the interviews for my work as a photo model, when I heard the drums of a belly dance on 30th Avenue.

I was struck by a pressing sound that had that rhythm that penetrates you, rushes through all parts of your body, and makes it hard to stay still. I felt like the music and the dance were in synch with my mind, my emotions, my inner rhythm.

It was a revelation for me. I felt that I was responding to a calling more than a discovery, so I went to see where the music was coming from.

The person who was playing the drum, Ahmed Hussein, became my first teacher. When I signed up for classes, he let me go to the school for free, because he knew that I was still struggling with my weekly rent. At the time, I was staying at a hotel called the Martha Washington, which offered me more security since it allowed only women.

As I progressed, I realized that I was losing weight without using any tricks, and that my relationship with my body was at ease. My metabolism was changing thanks to the movements that worked my abdomen. The dancing filled me with the joy and optimism I needed to face my difficulties, and it helped me keep my body in shape.

During lessons, Ahmed encouraged us to watch our bodies...not in the mirror to correct something or to compare ourselves to the other students...but to look directly at the thighs and the belly, and the hands that slowly moved around the body, seeming to caress the skin.

The attention he gave me as a teacher helped me learn to practice consistently, because if I missed a lesson, I had to give him an explanation. He helped me discover that I could always find a friend in dance.

Going to lessons, even when I really didn't feel like it, taught me that to succeed in an art, you'll get more results from constant practice than from that powerful, momentary stroke of creativity attributed to the muses who inspire artists.

And so I also persisted in the world of fashion, afflicted as it is by the idea that the normal height of a model should start at 5'9", which meant that the 3 inches I was missing kept me from getting the steadier and more rewarding jobs reserved for taller girls.

However, I was often able to make the cut, partly due to my dancing skills. One of a dancer's merits is that she knows her body well, and she knows how to move it. A model can be very tall, but this doesn't necessarily mean that she's coordinated. Some photographers prefer to work with dancers, not only because they have a refined sense of movement, but also because they have uninhibited and natural relationships with their bodies. This allows them to take sensual shots without seeming vulgar, and without wasting precious time when the modeling agencies are being paid by the hour.

The world of fashion, which thrives on physical appearance, made me consider what kind of impact my looks could have on others. I realized that this awareness could make me less vulnerable to being taken advantage of and that, on the contrary, my physical appearance was a gift that I could use to my own advantage.

I learned how to do my hair by myself and to do my make-up like a professional, which is different for color photos, black and white, TV and film. It was al-

> Going to lessons, even when I really didn't feel like it, taught me that to succeed in an art, you have to practice persistently...

You can always find space to practice at home!

so important in that not all clients come with hair and make-up artists, so knowing how to do it myself, I had a better chance of being chosen.

Listening to the parameters that the photographers used to choose the best pictures, which were usually narrowed down from hundreds to just one, I learned to appreciate the art of photography and I developed an eye looking at the composition of the pictures.

With a little perseverance, my portfolio filled up with professional photos.

Unfortunately, dance wasn't enough to make up for my missing inches, so my agent, trying to console me, told me that there was no minimum height requirement for being an actress. I immediately got ready to go to the meeting that she booked for the soap opera "Search for Tomorrow."

This first interview was very strange. During the audition something unexpected happened that made me feel like I had to apologize to the casting director who read the dialogue with me. My character was unjustly accused in court, and since I myself hadn't had the best relationship with the law, the situation made me lose my head and, as I was reading the part, I actually got really angry.

I was sure that my interviewer was going to send me away and complain to my agent about my behavior. But before I had a chance to speak, she told me that she was very happy to offer me the job and then she sent me to wardrobe to get the dress for the part!

That particular scene not only helped me free myself of a nightmare from the past, but it also gave me my first lesson in acting: "You can get away with murder," because when you play a part, your actions don't have the same consequences that they would in real life. But this doesn't mean that you can't cause harm to the other actors. Fortunately, in this case, the interviewer didn't take my outburst personally, because I was in character. I was just playing my role.

With the fortune of having a professional job, I was able to join the actors' union, and curious about this "game," I decided to look into it further.

Acting also brought me closer to another discipline very similar in principle to belly dancing: Hatha yoga.

I was chosen to work on a TV comedy with Ellen Burstyn, Oscar winner and director of the Actors' Studio. Working with Ellen was not only a great honor for me, but also an opportunity to grow as a person. She took preparation for acting very seriously and didn't limit it just to reciting a part. Rather, it involved the entire expressive being of a person. It was Ellen who introduced me to meditation and yoga. She herself practiced yoga, meditated, and followed breathing exercises before shooting a scene, because it helped her reach a very deep level of relaxation and gave her control over her skills, both physical and mental, which she later transformed into award-winning performances. At first, yoga and meditation seemed like exotic rituals to me, a little strange for my taste. But in time I learned how important they are. Yoga's unique breathing style, pranayama, allows you to reach an immense level of relaxation that coincides with an inner state of absolute clarity and love for life.

With Ellen Burstyn in New York, on the set of the sit-com "The Ellen Burstyn Show," where I played her student.

I learned that you should never stop studying or looking into new areas when you are curious. At one point, I ventured towards psychoanalysis, which offered me a magnifying glass in looking at my own hidden reasoning. If it weren't for my absolute necessity to have dancing in my life, I would have dedicated myself to psychoanalysis.

The TV advertisements that I did became nationally publicized and made it possible for me to study, travel, and live without great economic leaps. I had become good at dancing in any setting: from a magic carpet advertising an airline company, to the back of an elephant in a desert oasis that was supposed to make people want to drink Coke.

The fruits of my labor allowed me to work as an actress with a certain level of security, something that's unthinkable even for many American actors. I played a regular role in the soap opera "All My Children," appeared with Don Johnson on "Miami Vice", and worked with Quentin Tarantino in the film, "Reservoir Dogs". Even though violent movies make me feel uncomfortable, I have a nice memory of Quentin because he knew how to make his actors feel like a team, giving us secret suggestions on the set. More importantly, he really liked my accent, and for "*Reservoir Dogs*", he had fun recording my voice in Spanish as well.

Being a foreign actress, I didn't always have such good luck; my Spanish accent was a very tough obstacle to overcome. I took lessons in Standard English pronunciation, but to be honest, even when I really tried to lose my accent, deep down inside, I don't think I wanted to let go of it. This would have meant hiding the musical traces of my childhood.

I love my Spanish accent because it's tied to my origins and to my mother tongue.

My Spanish accent was a very tough obstacle to overcome.

Different advertisements I did in New York for Coca-Cola, a cosmetics line, and stockings

At the "Reservoir Dogs" party in Los Angeles, with the director, Quentin Tarantino; Tim Roth, who is joking around as always; the film's costume designer; and Steve Buscemi

I finally realized this when I went back to speaking Spanish to my newborn daughter, Martinica; it was a real joy. And also because it is the instinctual language I run back to when my children make me really mad and I have to scold them.

My children were born in Italy, which I had suspected would be the country for me, even before visiting. In addition to dancing, I also found love here one very hot day in June, when I met my husband, Calogero. It was after a belly dancing performance at the Academy of Egypt in Rome.

The first thing to strike me, the first time I visited Italy, was how warm the people are, which wasn't even possible to imagine in Hollywood. I had the sensation of coming home to live in a family atmosphere, with everyone reunited at a big table! It was a fascinating experience, and it moved me to the point that it made me say: "Ah, here I am…I'm finally home."

Maternity allowed my philosophy on belly dancing to grow in a big way. It allowed me to try a "dancing gestation period," which ended up uncovering the real meaning that dancing has for me. During my pregnancies I continued to follow my students. And at home alone, I improvised with slow music that helped me feel the babies. It was my secret, especially during my second pregnancy, when I was expecting twins and had a greater need for a solid anchor to help me overcome the natural fears and physical discomforts of my condition.

With my sisters, Alexandra and Ida, and my daughter, Martinica.

With Leandro, Gabriel, Martinica; my husband Calogero, and Federica.

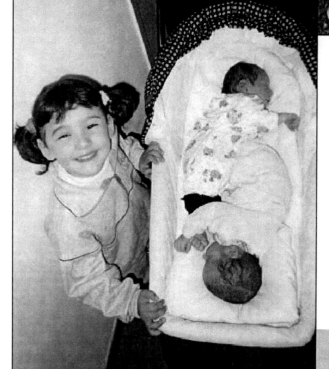

My Italian roots: little Martinica and the twins as they sleep together in the stroller.

Through dance, I opened myself up to life, which had already given me the eyes, ears, and mouth necessary to get by in the world. So you'll have to excuse me if my eclectic choreography makes your head spin a little.

I don't feel that I am so much a belly dancing "specialist" as I am a "generalist," because through this art, I have visited, and at times invaded, many different areas in which belly dancing is a hidden guest.

In my life, this has been the flowing dance that, after a long whirlwind, brought me where I wanted to end up: Here, Here, Here.....

I invite you to look closer at this dance, to get to know its secrets, and not to define the word *secret* as "recipe," because at the heart of it, it's the experience of belly dancing's sensual movements that every person can have, and that is the real source of its secrets.

The Practice of Belly Dancing

The following is a list of the most common themes regarding belly dancing, and the questions most frequently asked by people who are interested in this practice.

THE RIGHT BODY

The ideal body for this dance has nothing to do with sizes or measurements. Rather, it is the body of any woman who accepts her feminine traits, and who takes pleasure in looking at herself while she dances, feeling fluid, sensual, and happy to live in her own body. She doesn't search for constant verification in the mirror, in fashion, or in the tastes of others. The woman who is drawn towards belly dancing finds the beauty of her body in its graceful movement, in the creative life that the belly encloses, and in the bridge that it stretches out to bring us closer to others.

DIFFERENT MOTIVATIONS

Are there good reasons for choosing this type of dance?
Women come to my lessons with different motivations, from the most superficial: "It's very fashionable, so I want to try it," to the more profound: "I need to discover my femininity," or "I feel like it's the language for me." Personally, I don't give much value to these preliminary motivations. The important thing is that they offer the initial stimuli that inspire curiosity, because after some time spent getting to know the dance, these motivations can change, or new ones can be added, and little by little we uncover different aspects.

WHAT WILL PEOPLE SAY?

Sometimes it happens that women worry about what other people will think when they say that they're studying or dedicating themselves to belly dancing, especially in the "serious" workplace. If this is the case, I would like to suggest that, as with all things we hold dear, this be shared only with people who would appreciate it. As for me, over the years that I've worked as a professional dancer and instructor, I have become aware of all the clichés to which I can be subjected, and therefore, I have made an effort to behave in a way that is respectful of myself and of the dance that I study. I have lived through all the things that "people think" and any judgments that they might have passed about me. It is important, in any case, that whoever wants to dance professionally is creative and does her research on what the most appropriate venues for presenting the dance are: theaters, cultural associations, organizations that hold conferences, theme parties, and other places where you could find off-the-beaten-path forms of expression.

THE RIGHT AGE

There is no right age for this dance, because it doesn't force the body to do anything that it can't. You follow the rhythms of the body and its transformations.

We don't have to adapt ourselves to the technical demands of the dance; instead, the dance accompanies us, and follows us through life.

I have young students of 14 or 15, along with mature women of 50. Dancing helps the young girls pleasantly face the issues of their changing bodies, become familiar with themselves, be kind to themselves, and build a healthy body image based on the body itself. This helps them avoid the immediate and often depressing identifications with the media's models.

The older women and the mothers discover that with the passing years there are positive turns. Contrary to what they might have imagined, their dancing is more enriched, acquires more depth, and becomes more introspective. Over the years, we can accept and know our own sexuality better, and have a greater awareness of and control over the body's abilities.

To see positive results with this dance, we don't need to worry about age. I think a more important factor is that, in any stage of a woman's life, it is essential to have continuity both in practice and in the search that pushes us towards inner truth.

DANCING DURING PREGNANCY

It is advisable and there are no negative side effects for normal pregnancies. It's better to wait until the fourth month, and from that point until the end, you can follow an easy and fluid dance routine with a trained instructor. Many women describe belly dancing as the dance for mothers-to-be. It really is worth trying it to experience the possibilities that are reserved especially for women who are expecting.

THE RIGHT TEACHER

Many people wonder how to choose the right teacher. I think that it's important to have a certain flexibility to understand that the right kind of teacher (whether male or female) can change over time. Most often, the ideal person that we seek to guide us reflects the needs that we have during different periods of our maturation. However, our choice also reflects the needs created by the dance itself. If it is developed over time, with care, it becomes an ever-deepening and refined expression of our tastes and preferences.

I began studying dance at a very young age, and I have had many teachers; for belly dancing, I have had both male and female teachers, all of whom have taught me something valid. When I was young I preferred teachers who utilized very fast, spiking rhythms, and who gave me choreography to follow that I not only had fun with as I danced, but that also kept me in shape and developed my technique. That type of lesson was right for that particular purpose, at that time in my life, because I wouldn't have understood a style in which I wasn't completely covered in sweat at the end of the dance.

After years of working extensively on technique and choreography, I began to focus more on the content of the dance and on the feminine heritage that it holds. I interpreted the dance favoring the melody as if it were the mirror of my soul, moving my body slowly, and then adding in my breathing, calm and deep. That was an important time of growth for me, because with the slow cadence, I felt extremely vulnerable.

Improvisation also helped me a great deal, because I made myself open up to whatever the reality of the moment had to offer, using music that I had never heard before. And so, little by little, I got over my fear of not knowing what to do. It was as if everything that I had learned through my perseverance over many years of studying, and everything that I held in my "body memory" came together to form one language.

For this reason, it is important to try different teachers to be able to have a complete picture of the dance and to understand what style is the most agreeable for us.

However, I would like to ask you to watch out for the less-serious training that has developed in recent years, due to the popularity of belly dancing and the high demand for teachers. I think that the competence of someone who teaches an art depends on his or her professionalism and reasons for choosing to teach: the person could be driven purely by economic motivations, or (as we hope is the case) by a genuine desire to transmit his or her own knowledge freely.

Also, the expertise of a teacher should be the result of many years of study, not only of the dance itself, but also of the correct body positions to assume, as to avoid injuries. More importantly than teaching steps and how-to's, the instructor should inspire the student to get to know herself and to dance with joy and autonomy.

Finally, I think the right teacher should encourage us to practice regularly because without this, we can't even imagine possessing an art, much less dancing, which uses the body as its instrument.

FOR THE TEACHERS

I invite you to "dance between the lines," making use of all of the possible tools: different pieces of music, photos of painting and sculpture, books, poetry, etc. I suggest that you find a place in your lessons, between one step and another, to share your readings, and your intuitions with your students, without considering these moments when you're talking rather than dancing to be a waste of time. I'm sure that you will reap the benefits later, in the dancing itself, and in the renewed inspiration that your students will give your teaching.

THE MUSIC

Listening to different kinds of music is necessary to develop our preferences, dance well, and understand changes in rhythm and atmosphere.

Nowadays, you can find belly dancing CDs in every music store. It's helpful to listen to both the beat of the drums and the slow music of other instruments like the flute, the violin and the *qanun*. Next to the traditional belly dancing music, you can find the shelves of World Music with different CDs that lend themselves to belly dancing or dancing with a veil, and invite you to innovate and interpret.

LEARNING THE TECHNIQUE

In this book, I don't go into the techniques of dance very much. I don't think that a text book is the right way, because it's difficult to learn movements from descriptions in a book; obviously it would be better to take a course.

For first time learners, as well as those wanting to perfect their knowledge of the dance, I have made different didactic DVD's. They are dedicated to the technique of belly dancing's execution, and can be helpful in understanding how to do the steps,

"La Danza Orientale
risveglia le energie
più sottili delle
nostre emozioni.
I suoi movimenti
nascono quasi
spontaneamente
dal nostro
centro energetico,
liberando
dentro di noi
sensualità
e gioia".

CHOREO-GRAPHY OR IMPROVI-SATION?

how to position the body for different isolations, how to do a good shimmy and a fluid veil dance, and so forth. In any case, the physical part of dancing should go hand in hand with the introspective aspect that nourishes it.

Good training requires the utilization of both choreography and improvisation. Choreography and technique are important in understanding how the steps are done and how to put them together (transition). It's also important to test the different possibilities you have in utilizing the space. Choreography can provide evidence of a high level of expertise that goes along perfectly with every change in the music- since the movements are previously decided upon with recorded music- but this shouldn't be the end all be all to the dance. This way of looking at it can make us feel completely dependant on what we had planned beforehand and on the choreographer who tells us how to dance.

This approach makes us forget that the dance is inside of us and can be brought out little by little through the art of improvisation, which takes inspiration from what's going on at the moment. Choreography is refined improvisation.

Improvisation is a very important part in the study of this dance. I would say just as important as studying choreography and technique; however, it is often underrated in teaching. For many people, improvisation suggests something "put together," done at random, without preparation and without care.

Choreography and Improvisation are really like two sisters that work together: good choreography is rooted in an improvisational piece and shouldn't be limited to mechanically repeating the proposed steps, but rather requires the personal interpretation of the dancer following it. And improvisation is much more free, when we are familiar with the proper technique, execution of steps, and dynamic choreography that unfolds itself with the awareness of space, change in tempo, change in dynamics, and so forth.

It is important to be familiar with both choreographed and improvisational dance, and not to be afraid to try creating a dance on your own: we cannot box our dancing up to fit a CD where everything is already planned out. When we have the opportunity to dance to live music, in particular, a choreographed number might not hold up very well to the interpretation of the musicians, which can be very different than the music we have previously used in creating the choreography.

Group work is important in creating an atmosphere of cooperation and team-work. Dancers in the rehearsal studio at the Omphalos Theater (photo: C. Ferrara).

I think it's important to recognize that belly dancing originates as an *improvisational art*, if I may, followed at any given moment, using that which the moment presents to us, rather than something that has already been elaborated on.

THE GROUP

Group work is very important for us, because contrary to many types of women's groups where competition prevails, with belly dancing, there is usually an atmosphere of cooperation and team-work. It's true that this is not always the case, but I think that it is part of the teacher's responsibility to create a cooperative atmosphere in which the students feel comfortable expressing themselves through dance and sharing their likes and dislikes with the others. Above all, when working with improvisation, it is necessary to create a safe atmosphere where each person can reflect on their difficulties and growth with the others. Helping one another with the ups and downs, little by little they get over the fear of improvising and dancing in front of a group and allow themselves to express something personal. Improvisation becomes an interesting invitation that creates a bond for everyone as they try new things.

THE OMPHALOS THEATER IN ITALY

A good part of the practical work that this book is based on was developed during the workshops held at the Omphalos Theater near Rome, which is my creative space, the heart of my dance, the dream that is now coming true thanks to my husband Calogero and many valued contributors and artists such as the artist, Ettore De Conciliis. It is here that we dance, in a natural setting, on a stage that honors belly dancing as an art.

In the seminars that I run at the theater, I try to elaborate on technique and improvisation, but also on the ancient roots of this dance, which help us dance well: with intuition and spontaneity. With courage to follow our passions. The importance of the theater is confirmed when the dancers tell me, "It's easy to give my best here." At Omphalos you can dance without the usual constraints of other places that offer belly dancing lessons with makeshift stages or dancing among the tables, where it is very easy to lose the artistic and feminine benefits that belong to this dance.

Present Day Stereotypes and Forgotten Roots

For me belly dancing has always had a profound meaning: strength, pride, and respect for our femininity and for the female body; something much different from the clever, superficial appearances of the better part of belly dancing that is represented in night clubs, in the movies, or on TV. Far from being considered an art, belly dancing is still seen as an erotic exhibition by many people, aimed at a male audience for the most part. For many, it's still an exotic show coming from the Orient, that has been reduced to a dancer showing off her body in a dance that doesn't seem to require very accurate artistic preparation.

In all the countries where I've worked, the USA, Mexico, Italy, Egypt, Colombia, Japan, and Finland, these clichés are the same for the most part, and they are spread by the commercial use of belly dancing, more than by the will or motivations of the dancers.

Of course, you might happen to come across dancers who use their bodies in a vulgar way, and without much training, but these are isolated cases. Usually the dancers are very interested in learning about the different styles of the dance, in asking themselves about their roots, in seeing performances, in studying the drums and the cymbals, in looking for music that suits their taste, in improving their technique and interpretation with seminars and videocassettes: all of the things that finally translate into a great passion that the dancer develops with respect and devotion.

However, when belly dancing is brought to the public, something inevitably happens; it loses something. We are so often disappointed by how the dancing is seen or by what people expect of us as dancers. Because of this, it's important to understand what we can do to keep our dance alive as an art, and to take responsibility by saying "no" to the inappropriate use of what we do. We should be professional at all times and work with dedication, so that we will give people the complete picture of belly dancing. Therefore, in order to dance with deeper insight, it's good to be curious, to read, and to ask questions about the reasons that drive us to make this art part of our lives.

I will discus the language of symbols only in the second part of this book and there is a reason for this. From the beginning of my first drafts of the book, I felt it necessary to address the stereotypes that inevitably cohabitate with belly dancing, and that are strong and perpetuated by the media and by the different words we use to refer to the dance. Beginning with the vocabulary, I tried to bring to light the ideas and fantasies that we associate with different words. For example, what comes to

> Usually the dancers are very interested in learning about the different styles of the dance and in asking them selves about their roots.

mind when we hear the word "belly" or "Orient," ideas that feed into many of the stereotypes connected to belly dancing, in ways that we are sometimes unaware of. After this, I investigated the universal vision of the world that already exists on a deeper level, worthy of redemption and respect. I think that, as long as we lack an understanding of its true make up, belly dancing will remain a superficial art: a dance that is externalized with beautiful movements that are executed technically, but without the magic of the elements held deep inside. For me this dance has an extremely ample life, both in space and time that cannot be satisfied by the empty completion of two nice steps. And despite the difficulties that our dance faces as an art, I like to hope that it can still be revived through its original importance as a sacred dance of life and rebirth.

> I think that, as long as we lack an understanding of its true make up, belly dancing will remain a superficial art: a dance that is externalized with beautiful movements that are executed technically, but without the magic of the elements held deep inside.

The various interpretations of belly dancing that we know today have many roots. It's like a huge tree with different style-branches and influence-roots that nourish it. Of course, it's very hard to search for or speak about all the roots of this ancient dance. In this book, I focused on one root in particular, the one that I consider to be the deepest and most ancient source, that is able to unify the languages of this dance into a universal one: the Neolithic root, which brings us back to the idea of origins. It still communicates the symbols of life, regeneration, fertility, and birth through our bodies today. It is from the same school of thought, and from the cult that worshiped the Ancient European and Middle Eastern Goddesses, that our dance got its start.

In this book I propose some hypotheses that your own similar experience with belly dancing could either confirm or prove false. But the most important goal of this research on its symbols is to invite you to experience an aware movement of the body.

> I am convinced that belly dancing's language lives inside of us.

Belly dancing has become a part of me, and with it, I interpret the world around me and the world inside of me. It's an instrument that I sought out to get to the heart of our origins, the beginning of things, life itself, starting out from the belly, its symbols and its language. I am convinced that this language lives inside of us just as the symbols live inside the body and evoke a greater reality. I call this reality: the All, the Goddess, the Infinite. The dance is part of the All because it celebrates our sacred and sensual nature through the body and it sees life as a divine spark to be kept glowing.

The Absence of the "Feminine"

As a dancer who expresses herself through a mostly feminine language, I am used to looking for "keys," throughout the day, that could contribute to my work. This is a difficult job because usually the experiences of women and femininity are excluded from daily life and instead, the life of man takes precedence as a synonym for the universal human life. Try to pay attention and understand how exactly the feminine language is missing from many areas of life: linguistic forms, for example, are masculine, even when they refer to the woman; in the popular forms of dance offered to girls today, they use choppy and aggressive movements without giving importance to the natural, rhythmic, continuous movement of the body. Even with a typically feminine art such as belly dancing, most of the time it seems that we follow a frenetic sort of "oriental aerobics" that is not connected to our breathing and is based more on technique. And make no exception for the absence of the feminine in the monotheistic spiritual traditions, because God is defined only in masculine terms, while religious figures that praise *all the different aspects* of a woman's life are almost non-existent. And what should we say about a moment that could be considered the ultimate feminine experience, giving birth? Even during this experience we are pushed further away from our own nature, because many women feel that their instinct and knowledge of their own bodies are secondary to scientific resources.

In written history, the female point of view is usually absent: even in the word "history," the pronoun "his" refers to that which belongs to man, the man's story. To give another banal example, while I was working on this book, I typed the word "matriarchal" and the computer "corrected" me with the word "patriarchal," as if it only expected the male point of view!

In written history, the female point of view is usually absent...

The disappearance and the devaluation of the feminine symbolism in our culture are the foundation of the stereotypes about belly dancing. They have degraded our art and have impoverished the models that we base our work on, making negative framework even when we don't realize it.

To learn this dance it is important to understand the expressive capacity of our bodies through the movements and rhythm. It's also important to *remember* the steps, *remember* the dance as we take it from "herstory," the matriarchal heritage, in which *belly dancing plays a part*, as an art that, millennia after its birth, still possesses the symbols of an archaic feminine sacredness.
Recognizing a feminine feeling as something legitimate is important for everyone, because it is a beneficial strength inside us that we can count on and that we can share with others.
Every person has this treasure inside, even if it remains invisible in the rational environment of the workplace or in the hurried life of every day.
It is cultivated in a space that is dedicated to dance, that liberates us from many restraints, and that teaches us to value feminine strength, even in environments outside of the dance studio.
Its language gives us a voice in the world.
In my reconsidering of the feminine heritage, the proposal of a world seen only from the female point of view is not implicit; it wouldn't be possible nor fortunate, just as the world of our culture today is unfortunate. It is characterized by an extreme one-sidedness that has carried us forward in the fields of technology,

Recognizing a feminine feeling as something legitimate is important for everyone.

science, and organization, but that has separated us from nature and from the body's instincts with consequences that we know all too well.

Even if the status of women and of belly dancing were to change radically in our patriarchal society, it is not my intention to attack men as the ones responsible for their advantageous position, which is, in the end, detrimental to everyone. I don't think that personal growth can flourish by placing blame on others, but instead, by using our time and energy to create real possibilities through art and culture.

I speak mainly to women here because belly dancing gives privilege to the feminine principles and is centered around the physical and spiritual strength characteristic of woman. However, the themes that inspire it don't have a gender, and the awareness that we can gain by changing our conceptions can benefit everyone around us, including men.

The Ancient Egyptian hieroglyph that represents humanity is very beautiful. Woman and man who form one whole.

As I write, I also think about the men who are sensitive to art and nature, who could certainly be interested in knowing the inherent philosophy of belly dancing and the "feminine mysteries," not to mention the benefits in their relationships with others. I wish for them to find the opportunity every now and then to dance with their partners.

I believe that it is also important for a couple to value the moments dedicated to themselves as individuals, to explore their own interests, as belly dancing might be for a woman. It can help keep the flame of love burning over time.

As the poet says:

> «*Sing and dance together and be joyful,*
> *But let each one be alone:*
> *Even the chords of the lute are alone*
> *Though they vibrate to the same music*».

> *K. Gibran*

Introduction: Current Stereotypes and Forgotten Roots

The Inner Mirror

As a teacher and a dancer, I think it is important to discus the influence of the external appearance of our bodies, because it has to do with the pleasure that we perceive and the pleasure that we think it can inspire in other people. I inevitably face this issue during my lessons, because we are so bombarded with messages about what a beautiful, seductive body should look like, that it's difficult for a woman to feel up to par with these examples. Sometimes it is this exact fear of not being good enough that keeps many women from dancing even though they would like to try. I often hear people say, "I'm too fat," "I'm too thin," "I'm old," "My breasts are non-existent," "…. and I think I can dance?" Yes! Try it! Who knows where dancing will take you…this is my response.

Even if all forms of dance utilize the mirror as a didactic instrument, I make it a habit to draw the students' attention away from it during lessons, to position themselves in a way that they are not constantly tempted to look at it. The use of a mirror gives the idea that the dancer can concentrate better on what she's doing, but in reality I think it pushes her further away from herself, her real center, and from feeling her movements with pleasure. It is a tool that points out visual stimuli that often reflect a very critical image that we have of ourselves and can establish or contribute to competitiveness within the group rather than cohesion.

Of course, the mirror can be helpful, but it should be used in moderation and it shouldn't replace our inner mirrors.

The mirror as a window to our inner conscience, provides us with a non-judgmental gaze and should take precedent over the physical mirror that we find in front of us. This challenge of looking inward by listening to the body's sensations, to our desires, and to our breathing is important, not only for beginners, but also for those who have been dancing for years, especially for those who have not had the chance to focus on "the inside," to feel the force and the power of the belly.

During the seminars, we practice the movements with our eyes closed and we try to understand them based on the sensations that tell us how the body uses its space and what to do with a specific piece of music as we feel it personally, intimately. At this point, the mirror becomes an accessory, in the sense that it doesn't have to be a constant fixation in order for us to look for answers. These can be brought out by developing the internal gaze. From this prospective, the dance also gives us the ability to define ourselves, because it doesn't depend exclusively on the external elements to which we often turn for confirmation on how we look: like the effect of the stare, both ours in the mirror, as well as the stare of the other people who watch us.

Feeling an inner mirror is important for women in general, because the female body is the favorite target of the media's manipulation, which tells us how we should look,

From this prospective, the dance also gives us the ability to define ourselves, because it doesn't depend exclusively on the external elements to which we often turn for confirmation how we should behave, how we should move. Much more so in the performance industry where these manipulations are proposed as improvements for work.

In Los Angeles, for example, plastic surgery is very common, particularly in the world of cinema and television, which focuses on physical appearance, on the visual impact of the body, which is well-exercised, blown up in all the "right" places, homogenized and unsanctified. Breast implants are just the beginning of a long list of operations that many of my co-workers, actresses and dancers, undergo, because they consider them to be important to their survival in the world of show biz. These surgeries are justified by the film and TV industries to the point that a professional dancer can deduct the cost from her taxes along with the other work related expenses.

This touched up female model feeds into the global imagination and is thereafter exported worldwide through Hollywood's films and TV programs.

To tell the truth, it's not my intent to pass negative judgment about the surgical operations carried out on adult women. I am glad that we are able to choose what happens to our own bodies. However, I don't consider the implicit message of surgery to be very kind to us: it suggests that we are missing something and that we should run to get it repaired, even if there are risks involved, to make the "right body" come out, one that is worthy of our love and of others' appreciation.

> **As wrapped up as we all are in the patented images of beauty versus ugliness...belly dancing comes as an antidote to these poisons, asking us to discover the intrinsic value of our bodies just as they are.**

As wrapped up as we all are in the patented images of beauty versus ugliness, we go on living our lives worrying excessively about our physical appearance. Here the message of belly dancing comes as an *antidote* to these poisons, asking us to discover the intrinsic value of our bodies *just as they are*, and to define our sensuality, our *sex appeal*, not by the measurements of isolated parts of the body, but through the pleasure of moving every part, and the discovery of the secret power that exists within the body.

Dancing is an assertive art that can make us understand that we don't need external interventions, like surgery, extreme diets, or the mirror's confirmation to make us more desirable or happier. The movements of belly dancing aim at helping us discover the body's hidden sensuality, not only seeming "sexy," but also realizing its possibilities, *concentrating on its strong points* not on what is "missing."

> **Belly dancing is very feminine because it praises a body with a rotund form.**

Belly dancing is very feminine because it praises a body with a rotund form. But it doesn't impose an ideal physical model on us. Even though it's true that the movements are more visible with a full figure, the thing that counts the most is how the woman inhabits her body, how she communicates her individuality.

Introduction: Current Stereotypes and Forgotten Roots

Part One

CHAPTER I

What would you like to call your dance? The "right" name for it

The key to understanding belly dancing's hidden language can be found in its many different names. For this reason, I ask the women in my courses to choose the name that they prefer for to use. I tell them that in the spirit of ancient Egyptian belief, the verb "nourish" and "name" are inseparable, because to give a name was to nourish a being, allowing it to develop. By making an effort to understand the different content of the names, we are able to realize how the dance is a dynamic art that, in order to stay alive, depends on whatever each individual has to offer. It grows through the exchange of opinions. Naming, or more appropriately, renaming the dance, we call something into a *conscious existence*. During this debate, the women explain their choices and their reasons, and it might even be the first time that their curiosity is peaked about the different names. I believe that it's important to reflect on and to be well-informed of the implications of every name-- because there are different stereotypes attached to each one-- in order to choose the one that is most compatible with our individual ideas and experiences, and to avoid passively using any old name at random.

Even though I must admit that it gives me pleasure when they share my point of view and understand the specific reasons that brought me to use the name "belly dancing." I don't want to lead my students into making the same choice that I did. I believe that it's important to encourage research, and that it's constructive when a person has a different point of view and actively develops her own vision. This allows us to see other aspects of the dance. So it happens that sometimes the dancers choose a name that isn't heard very often, or one in another language. There are different names for different women, and by making a conscious and well-informed choice, they begin to create their own dance, and to nourish it, even in this less obvious aspect. As I tell my students, "It's your dance. Choose, with care, the name that best represents it in your eyes."

The fact that belly dancing "escapes" being classified under just one name, and that its steps are very difficultly catalogued under just one "code," shows the many points of view that it embodies. This multifacetedness is, in a way, like the different interpretations we can give to the words of a poet, which speak to the sensitivity of the heart and elude the calculations of reason. For every dancer, the name should be drawn out of her emotional experience of the dance, from what she truly feels about "the Orient," or "belly," "raks sharky," or "belly dance," or even about "the Middle East," but it should also come from the awareness of the cultural implications of these different names.

In choosing a name, we can become more aware of the hidden values, or the values that have disappeared, in order to give a more personal meaning to the dance. In this way it becomes personal, even when we "dig up" the various implications of the names and when we refuse to yield to the stereotypes.

But what do the different names suggest? What do other people have in mind, even before the dancer makes a move?

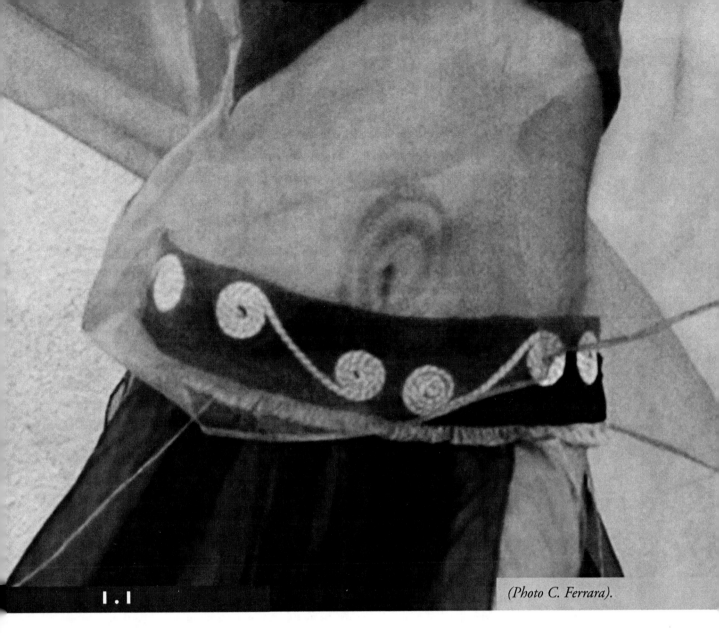

(Photo C. Ferrara).

1.1

What Belly
for Belly Dancing?

*«People go around the world now, hardly remembering
that they possess a body and in it, life, and we're afraid,
the world is afraid of the words that denominate the body…».*

P. Neruda, Residence on Earth.

Let me begin with the most common name for our dance, "belly dancing." This name is not always ideal for the dancers, because "belly" might seem like too narrow of a word for those who are familiar with the dance's virtue and who know that it uses every single part of the body. More importantly, this name creates discomfort because right away it puts into question a part of the female body that is subject to various misconceptions.

In fact, the most common ideas linked to the word "belly" are negative, for the most part, because usually we associate it with primal and animalistic acts. "Belly," in our western culture, is synonymous with "paunch" and "animal appetite," which belong to the reality of the inferior, terrestrial world represented by the body, as opposed to the superior, spiritual world located above, in the heavens and in our heads.

We are expected to give value to our rational abilities, a fact which allows a certain vilification of the central part of the body, of the belly and of the bond we have with the earth. In fact, when we want to affirm that something is commonplace, we use the word "mundane," which comes from the Latin *mundus* meaning "world".

What happens to the belly when we dance? In many different styles of dance, we require our bodies to keep a tight control over the belly, making it "disappear," or we lock it rigidly into place, not only to give proper support to the spinal column, but for other less obvious reasons.

I felt this kind of control over my body when I was young and first dedicated myself to dancing professionally. Exploring the different styles, I always felt the need to fight against the roundness of my belly. When I studied classical dance, we were told to suck our stomachs in and hold them there. The belly disappeared while the rest of the body was free to move. In my modern dance lessons at the Martha Graham school, the abdominal movements could be best described as contractions that aimed at pulling the belly completely inward, creating a sort of bas-relief out of the body.

It was only later with belly dancing, when I timidly rolled my warm-up pants down to my hips, leaving my belly uncovered, that I finally had the sensation that this part of the body could also move freely, vibrate, express emotion, and have a roundness to its shape. I loved it! My belly had woken up.

**I loved it!
My belly
had woken up.**

Part of the role of belly dancing, which celebrates the procreativity of the female belly as its name suggests, is to uproot the various "mental corsets." Just like the corsets that were wrapped around women's bodies in the 1800s, mental cor-

What Belly for Belly Dancing

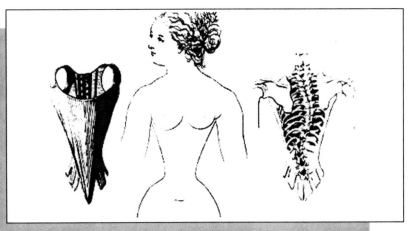

The aesthetic ideal of the corset in the Victorian era, the form that it was supposed to give the woman's body, and the terrible consequences on the spinal column, respiration, and the out-of-place ribs. Belly dancing was the exact antithesis of this ideal, because it praised a belly free of restriction, and therefore was presented as an art against the norm.

sets can also constrict our bodies. And this is the reason that pushes many women to learn more about belly dancing.

These mental corsets are hidden in today's aesthetic ideal of the female body, which is not a rotund body with soft, feminine curves, or a "terrestrial" body, close to the earth. On the contrary, it's a long and lean body that stretches away from itself, reaching upwards, challenging gravity. The belly, in its attempt to elude the earth, has disappeared. It's a belly that has been denied.

From a very young age girls learn to force their bellies to be still: holding the stomach in and breathing only with the upper part of the chest, using thoracic respiration.

This blockage is not only of concern to the physical being, but also to the emotional one, because the two are closely related. The barrier put up around the belly also isolates the "uncomfortable" emotions, such as anger, sadness, and pain, even though they are just as important a part of life as joy. But we learn as children to repress our discomfort and to shut it inside the body, which often times can translate into symptoms of illness and disease later on.[1]

The revealed body proposed by the Western world of fashion tells us that the belly is free and out in the open. But this is only how it appears to be; it takes a lot more than a cropped shirt or low-rise jeans to live in your skin with pleasure and with taste. We still have a good amount of work to do, because we were born into a culture that refuses to see the spirituality of the body, that over the centuries has denigrated more than celebrated the characteristics of the belly as a source of life and creativity.

This obsessive control over the female belly is not a prerogative of the Western world alone; it exists in the Middle East as well. We can see it in the very dance that has celebrated the woman's body for millennia, and it is confirmed by the caged-in bellies of the belly dancers who are required by law to keep the zone in question completely covered by the fabric of their costumes. In Egypt, for example, they risk high fines if they dance in public with their bellies revealed. But how did we become so afraid of the belly? To the point where we want absolute control over its functions, where we don't consider a round belly to be

The revealed body proposed by the Western world of fashion tells us that the belly is free and out in the open. But this is only how it appears to be.

full of life and emotion..? I think it's important to take a look at the myths and philosophies that have inspired our culture and at the history that has done a great deal to eliminate or to control the belly and the uterus within it. This will help us realize that even today, after millennia, a women is expected to reflect these images that are so averse to the female body, that prevent her from living with the center of her body as a starting point, that chip away at her ability to make decisions about her own body.

After that, in the chapter on the symbolism of the belly, we'll take a look at the positive traits of this symbol, which give an invigorating meaning back to the name "belly dancing." But first I would like to present the significance of the belly that we have inherited from history.

WORK CITED IN CHAPTER 1.1

1.A. Lowen, *La spiritualità del corpo.*

1.2

The Emptied
Out Belly

«Since the female body has the great gift of nourishing,
developing, and bringing an heir into the world,
the control of every society,
modern or ancient, passes through her body».

D. Maraini, La nave per Kobe, diari giapponesi di mia madre.

The procreative heritage of belly dancing has been around for ages. It precedes the monotheistic religions and dates back to the workship of the Goddesses and their symbols. For both our dance and the ancient religion, the focal point is the procreativity of the female body, and thus, the symbol of the belly is very important. It was exactly because of its significance that it became the target of an extreme and contradictory transformation in the myths of Creation and in the monotheistic religions, Judaism, Christianity, and Islam. These religions aimed to establish their supremacy, and therefore worked to either eliminate the previous religious cults or to incorporate them into the new religions.
During this time of transformation, the symbol of the belly lost all of its ancient sacredness, and stopped associating the woman's body with the metaphors that were meant to reinforce life.

Jesus saw women for all their dignity

Of course with Christianity, if we take the teachings of Jesus Christ alone, we find it encouraging to know that he saw women for all their dignity. However, before Christ, woman, along with her belly, had definitely already been put in her place, as we can see in the first part of the Old Testament. The book of *Genesis* and the story of Original Sin were already as well-known then as they are now[1].
In the Old Testament, the generative beauty of the belly is no longer spoken about. Instead, there are references to Astarte (the Bible's condensed version of the "Utero Goddesses" Ishtar and Anat) as the bearer of Satan. Even the vowel sounds of her name were inserted in such a way as to obtain the precise meaning of "something shameful."[2] This change is not to be taken lightly, since in the older lunar religions, the symbol of the belly held within it the capacity to create and give, and was the source of power and charisma for women.

...women's natural ability to give life was taken away from her and reassigned to the male.

In the stories of creation, both in the Bible and the Koran, we can see a reversal in the gender roles when women's natural ability to give life was taken away from her and reassigned to the male. It was no longer the belly of the Goddess to give life, but rather the mouth of God, through his word: In the beginning there was the word (John); And God said "let there be light, and there was light." And Even in the Islamic religion, "When Allah makes a decree, he just says 'be' and it is" (Koran XX). In *Genesis*, there are two different stories about the creation of woman. In the first, God brings her to life at the same time as man (1:27), but then a few lines down, in a more detailed account, which is the one with more echoes through history, woman is formed out of the rib bone of man- a little riblet woman- and not born from a mother's belly. (*Genesis* 1:27).

The formation of every population also starts with a single man: Israel descended from Abraham, who begot his son (born from a slave girl--a secondary fact), who begot another son, and so it goes on to form the lineage of the Arabic people.

The womb of the first mother, Eve, is cursed and condemned to experience pain during childbirth (*Genesis* 3:16). The serpent, a symbol of the earlier Goddesses, is condemned to slither the earth and eat dust.

The belly, as a symbol of all that is feminine, doesn't make a come back in the legend about our origins. It is always seen as evil incarnate, the instrument by which suffering and sin came into the world. To speak the truth, I don't think the importance of the belly ever makes a come back, even when the Christians affirmed that this "stain" was washed clean by the virginal womb of Mary, mother of God. The virginity of Mary is considered to be a virtue, a physical trait, while the virginity of the Goddesses in the ancient religions was perceived very differently. They were considered to be at one with themselves, and this was a concept that stemmed not from the woman's physical condition, but from her self-determination, her ability to choose her own destiny.

The model of the virgin Mary is that of a woman who becomes a mother while still remaining a virgin, since she "hadn't known a man," and she "conceived with vulva and uterus closed." She didn't even have to give a contribution of herself, other than welcoming into her womb the "perfectly formed and sanctified spirit and body of Jesus."[3] As a symbol of the feminine, the Virgin Mary's belly is a contradictory reflection with which women cannot identify completely, nor take any reinforcement from. With this example, we lack the positive references to the female belly as a creator of life, to menstruation, to sexuality, and to childbirth.

The belly of the first mother, Eve, is cursed and condemned to feel pain during childbirth.

Forgotten Traces of the Sacred Belly

The worship of Mary, a strong force in the Christian world, reflects the human need to redeem the feminine aspect of God, and demonstrates that this cannot escape the people's awareness.

Within the figure of the Christian Virgin are hidden the ancient Goddesses of fertility. Mary, like many of the mother Goddesses before her, brought a god of human form into the world, who then gives his life in order to save mankind, and then finally rises again.[4] This inherited story is almost tangible thanks to the iconographic image of the Virgin holding baby Jesus in her arms, which was originally inspired by the Goddess Isis with her son Horus in arm. Other traces of Uterine Goddesses crushed by the Bible stories are buried in many symbols

The Madonna with Milk, c. 1300. Lorenzetti.

The Goddess Iside breastfeeding her son Horus.

of today's religions. For example, Aserah and Ishtar, who inspired that "worship of life," belly dancing, can still be recognized in certain aspects of the modern religions. These passages found in Genesis 49 and 25 provide other examples:

"...they blessed the breasts (sadajim) and womb (raham)..." Both are symbols of the Goddess Aserah in the context of a mother Goddess. *Raham*, which literally means "maternal womb," was a symbol redressed with sacredness in Ugarit (an ancient city discovered in Syria in 1929, where tablets with writings about the Goddess were found dating back to 1400 BC) and was one of the names of Aserah/Athirat.[5]

Again in *Luke* 11:27, where positive symbols of the Goddesses live on in disguise: "As he said this, a woman in the middle of the crowd raised her voice and said 'blessed is the womb that bore you and the breast from which you drank milk'"

In the Koran, there are also traces of the ancient symbolism of the Goddess's sacred belly. For example, in the words that are used to address Allah, the merciful: the bismillah (the beginning words of the Islamic ritual, which opens the suras (chapters) of the Koran and that the Muslims use when they begin to recite their prayers) has the same linguistic base as "uterus" or "womb," and was a symbol, just as in the Bible, that became reassigned to the male figure when the Islamic religion was coming into existence.

In the Koran, there are also traces of the ancient symbolism of the Goddesses' sacred belly.

This archaic symbolism is also hidden in some Arabic words: batn (belly) which represents the clan or tribe, umm (mother) which refers to the Muslim community, and haya, which simultaneously refers to life and the female reproductive organs, and also expresses the belief in the belly as the sacred fulcrum of Life.

The *Occult* Omphalos

Along with the symbol of the belly, there are also many other symbols that were hidden under the cloak of history or the monotheistic religions. Originally they had a sacred, feminine value and were considered to be centers, or *omphalos*, fulcra of divinity. The *omphalos* was the connection between the heavens and earth, the highest point of land, and just as the sacred mountains were at one time symbols of the Goddess's belly, this was the earth's navel. In the Islamic tradition, it is the Ka'ba, which is supposed to be situated in front of the heavens' center.[6] Here one can find the intriguing guardian Black Stone of Mecca (perhaps a meteorite), the ancient symbol of the Goddess Al-Uzza, who along with the Goddesses Al-Lat and Menat, composed the great triad worshiped by the ancient Arabs.

In the Islamic religion, just as in the archaic religion of proto-Israel, the Goddesses were a part of the initial cult which only later became completely monotheistic. Ashera was the consort of the Old Testament God, Yahweh[7] and the Goddess Al-Uzza was adored by the same Mohammed (founder of the Islamic religion) as the Goddess of the desert, the Morning Star, the "powerful one." She was also the guardian of the priestesses in her sanctuary, which was situated among the Acacia trees in the south of Mecca. Generations of followers assembled at the site to worship her. Some time later, despite her devotion, he revolted against her. Even though he originally declared the worshipping of these three feminine figures to be lawful, as intermediaries of Allah Mohammed, later he destroyed the sanctuaries and denied any spiritual value in worshipping the Goddesses.[8] In the new religion, the ancient female element disappears completely, and it is believed that the Black Stone was brought to Abraham by the archangel Gabriel.

Today, the Ka'ba is guarded by the men who have inherited this position from the ancient priestesses. They are called "Beni Shaybah," which means "sons of the Old Woman." The characteristic "old" is one commonly used for the moon, a feminine symbol which corresponds to the three phases of a woman's life. The Beni Shaybah are descendents of the old women who carried out the same duty in ancient times.[9]

Another forgotten root that recalls the sacred dance of the past lies in the Muslim name for the pilgrimage to Mecca, hag, the root word at the base of this term indicates "dancing," or "circling" around something sacred.[10]

However, the human navel is a symbol that has brought about many uncertainties, even in the Christian religion. It is praised in the *Song of Songs*, the strangest book to be found in the Bible, which due to its erotic content, risked being omitted from the list of sacred texts. In any case, the navel remains an "uncomfortable trace" of a matriarchal past. The Song is a hymn of amorous desire between two people simply called the bride and groom. It is a song that praises the land and the fertile graces of the dancer, Solomon:

> The *omphalos* was the connection between the heavens and earth, the highest point of land.

> ...the navel remains an "uncomfortable trace" of a matriarchal past.

«Your thighs are turned out like jewels,
The handy work of a true master.
Your navel is a round cup that
Overflows with scented wine,
Your belly is a pile of grain surrounded by lilies,
Your breasts like two fawns, twin gazelles».

Song of Songs VII, 3.

Of the many possible translations available from the original Hebrew, I am most partial to one that preserves the matriarchal model proposed by Suares and cited by W. Buonaventura.[11] This interpretation, based on the "Code of the Kabala," observes that the word *yerekh*, for example, can mean both "thigh" and "hip," Furthermore, Suares explains that the translation of *hhalaeem* to "jewels" as we find in the orthodox Bible is inappropriate because the root of *hhalaeem* is hhal, which means "to fall, dance, quiver, or tremble." Thus instead of "your thighs shaped like jewels" he uses the interpretation, "the curves (or circular movement, speaking about the person dancing) of your hips seem to torment them (quivering or trembling), which reveals a sacred dance, sensual and favorable for fertility and birth.

The name Solomon may be reminiscent of the Goddess Ishtar since her temple was in Shulman, and since the varied vocabulary used to describe her movements is full of references to circularity, appropriate for the act of belly dancing, as well as a women's contortions during labor and childbirth.

Solomon's belly button is mentioned in the verses, and in Hebrew, it could have different meanings: limit, confines, pubic area, the gateway between two worlds, and most significantly, the sacred zone.

The dancer's belly button rises like a sacred and vital center, just as in the activities related to it, procreation, sexuality, and birth.

In this light, the dancer's belly button rises like a sacred and vital center, just as in the activities related to it, procreation, sexuality, and birth.

As a praise to life and eroticism, slipped into a contrasting environment, the navel is not neglected by the wisdom of Shahrazad who loads it with sensuality in the stories of *A Thousand and One Nights (Arabian Nights)*:
"Her throat looked like that of an antelope and her breasts, two pomegranates…and her belly button could have held an ounce of benzoic ointment," and even later, as she whispers into the king's ear as he falls asleep, "His navel could collect and ounce of musk, the most exquisite of perfumes."[12]

However, beyond inspiring love and desire, the belly button has always been an annoyance for the leaders of the church, because it is a symbol that draws us back to our origins, and in a certain way, it tarnishes our concept of God. The artists of the past had the dilemma of whether or not to include it in their paintings of Adam. According to the literal interpretation of the Creation, Adam was created directly by God, and it wouldn't have been possible for him to bear the unmistakable sign of being born from a woman.

In 1752, the German doctor, Christian Ephrain, concluded that Adam didn't have a belly button because he wasn't born, but rather, created: "Whoever doubts this is not a worthy member of the Church and should be signed over to the devil," or rather into the hands of the Inquistion.[13]

Then arose the problem regarding the similarity between Adam and God: if Adam had a belly button and was created in the image and likeness of God, then God must have had one too. But from here sprung a delicate question: who gave birth to God? In the Islamic religion, an ancient legend about the devil resolves the problem. After Allah had created the first man, the devil, enraged, spat upon the new creature. His spit struck the middle of the man's body. Allah immediately wiped away the dirty spot to prevent any contamination from spreading, and he left a small mark where the devil's spit had stricken the man. That sign became the first navel.[14]

The belly button represents our sexuality. The whole abdominal zone has an erotic charge strengthened by its proximity to the genitals, and this makes it an area to be censured. This is especially true of the navel, because it seems like a bodily orifice and has an "echo of genitalia," the real orifices located just below it.[15]

To avoid this uncomfortable subject, even at the start of the twentieth century, the navel was still being touched up and the belly appeared completely smooth in the first photographic images.

But how could belly dancing hide or camouflage the navel, since its suggestive twisting of the pelvis, exalts it and puts it at the center of attention?

The belly button represents our sexuality.

The harem as seen and interpreted in Hollywood during the 50's, with belly buttons strictly covered. For Vincent Minnelli's film, Kismet.

The "problem" was resolved by "Shera," Hollywood's Shahrazad, when belly dancing became popular in the 1940's and 50's. She covered the questionable area with fabric or with a jewel placed inside. In this way, she avoided being censored or accused of immorality and, perhaps without knowing it, recreated the ancient custom of adorning the center of the body, still characteristic of the dance today.

The Belly as Seen by Philosophers and Scientists

The fear and rejection of the belly was not characteristic of monotheism alone, but also of science, which set its weightiest pillar on Greek philosophy. In the Greek pantheon, we can find images of the original mother; to point out the religious equivalent, this would be Eve's counterpart. According to mythology, her name was Pandora (as told by Hesiod around the middle 8th century B.C.), the woman who spread pain throughout the world at the beginning of time. She opened the cover of her box (a symbol of the womb) and introduced evil to humanity.

The belly, as a mere container that acts as a host for living matter, has been brought down through history by the poet Aeschylus as well. In the *Eumenides* he gives these words to Apollo, bringing paternal authority and reason to life: «Not the true parent is the woman's womb that bears the child: She doth but nurse the seed new-sown; the male is parent; She for him, as stranger for a stranger, hoards the germ of life, Unless the god its promise blight». (as translated by Morshead)

However, the influence that most profoundly affected Western thought and the Church's official position on the female belly and human reproduction was the philosophy of Aristotle (4th century B.C.). In his work, *Generation of Animals*, Aristotle maintains that the woman provided the materials for the embryo and that the man gave these materials form and movement. At first glance, it could seem that this theory gives the woman an important role; however, in the Greek mentality of that time, which didn't have an appreciation for material things, that role was considered animal-like and inferior, while the male served the spiritual and infinitely superior function of giving life. For Aristotle, the woman is an inferior creature and is, at best, only good for her incubating services in mankind's fertility.[17]

Thomas Aquinas accepted the Aristotelian point of view in regards to woman's role in society, which considered man to be the vital source of life and woman simply the incubator. This point of view was then tailored and elaborated on by Dante, who described woman as having a passive virtue while man represented the active virtue (*Purgatory*, Canto 25,47).

Aristotle maintains that the woman provided the materials for the embryo and that the man gave these materials form and movement.

The marginalization of women on the natural events of reproduction served as a basis of the misguided interpretation of biological processes as well, according to which, her contribution was not essential to the creation of a new life. Seneca wrote in the 1st century A.D. in his famous discussion on physics, *Natural Questions*, "In the seed are enclosed all of the body parts of the man that will be formed. The infant born from the maternal womb has the roots of a beard and hair that one day will sprout out. In this little mass, there are also all of the features of the body, and everything else that posterity will discover in the man."

The philosophers that left their mark on human thought, such as Plato and Empedocles, made exactly this hypothesis, that later would be called preformism: the uterus, according to the preformists, was only the terrain in which the seed grew, and the sex of the child was determined by which side the menstrual blood fell on. This theory was pleasing to the Church, because it implied that the entire human race was created by God in the loins of Adam. The medieval Church maintained that a miniscule homunculus perfectly formed, complete with a soul, was deposited by the male into the body of the female, who worked only as the incubator.[18]

Paracelsus, considered to be among the best scientists of the 16th century and the founder of pharmaceutical chemistry, had already dreamt of being able to create an artificial man. In the first of his *Nine books of the nature of things*, he affirmed that it was possible to produce a homunculus or artificial man:[19] all you had to do was to let some human sperm sit in a jar of horse excrement for a period of forty days or until it began to take life and move around.

The uterus inspired some of the most grotesque ideas, offensive to woman, to her body, and to her femininity. Plato defined the uterus as an animal inside an animal, and in his *Timaeus*, he stated that the uterus was like an animal busy raising its young, and if it was not fertilized for a long period of time during the opportune season, it would get angry and rage through the whole body. Even the Hippocratic doctors were convinced that the uterus was able to pass through the diaphragm and reach the throat, something that was considered catastrophic for centuries. There was even an ecclesiastical formula in existence that addressed the uterus saying, "why do you get angry, why do you run here and there like a dog, why do you jump like a rabbit?[20]

The manifestation of this wandering uterus developed into the symptoms of hysteria, and for centuries, women were forced into submission because of this gossip. It is true that they were persecuted, tortured and burned on pyres to negotiate with the demons inside of them.

And what can we say about the 18th century theory, based on Aristotle, that maintained that the woman was really an inside-out man, with her reproductive organs developed on the inside instead of the outside of the body, but nevertheless the same as those of a man?

> The medieval Church maintained that the woman's body worked only as an incubator.

> An 18th century theory, based on Aristotle, maintained that the woman was really an inside-out man.

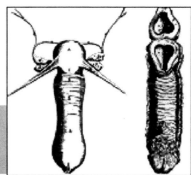

Anatomic depiction of the vagina in two 16th century tables, based on the Aristotelian philosophy that woman was an inside-out man, with reproductive organs identical to those of a man, but developed inside the body.

Belly dancing came as an art "against…"

In the Victorian era, the female belly was held tightly into the dress under the bust. They weren't allowed to speak about the belly, but only about the stomach, the area furthest away from the genitals.[21] It was said that the culture let the female reproductive organs waste away, and that giving women rights resulted in "insane asylums in every county and a divorce court in every city." Women were subject to having the clitoris and ovaries removed, as a curative measure for "forms of agitation," "suicide attempts," and "exotic tendencies."[22]

It was at that time in history that the Western world began to talk about belly dancing, which came as an art "against": against the status quo, against the ideas accepted from history, against the restrictions and feminine ideals in the world of fashion.

WORKS CITED IN CHAPTER 1.2

1. G. Bechtel, *Le quattro donne di Dio.*
2. P. Monaghan, *Le donne nei miti e nelle leggende.*
3. M. Warner, *Sola tra le donne.*
4. S. Husain, *La Dea.*
5. M. Baldacci, *Prima della Bibbia. Sulle tracce della religione arcaica del proto-Israele.*
6. M. Eliade, *Trattato di storia delle religioni.*
7. M. Baldacci, *Prima della Bibbia.*
8. P. Monagham, *Le donne nei miti e nelle leggende.*
9. E. Harding, *I misteri della donna.*
10. M. Baldacci, *Prima della Bibbia.*
11. W. Buonaventura, *Il Serpente e la Sfinge.*
12. M. Chebel, *Il libro delle seduzioni.*
13. T. Reik, *Psicoanalisi della Bibbia.*
14. D. Morris, *Il nostro corpo.*
15. D. Morris, *Il nostro corpo.*
16. J. Voss, *La luna nera.*
17. S. Nuland, *I misteri del corpo.*
18. A. Rich, *Nato di donna.*
19. S. Nuland, *I misteri del corpo.*
20. S. Nuland, *I misteri del corpo.*
21. D. Morris, *Il nostro corpo.*
22. A. Rich, *Nato di donna.*

The most famous dancer at the World Fair in Chicago in 1893, "Little Egypt." Sometimes identified with Fahreda Mahzar, sometimes with Ashea Wabe, she was of Syrian origin and had a strong and rebellious character. Because of the Chicago Fair, belly dancing came to the Western public and influenced the vision of the new style of dance: modern dance (photo used with kind permission of D. Carlton).

1.3

A Liberating Distortion

The term "belly dancing" was initially coined in the 19th century by Western travelers who went to the Orient. The free movement of the pelvis left a strong impression on them, but they watched the dance with judgmental eyes, and described it with adjectives like "shameful," "voluptuous," "wild," or even "stupid."[1]

If many women today think twice before talking about their passion for belly dancing, it is partly because even now it has a certain shocking quality. We can only imagine the effect it had on the Victorian population when they first discovered a dance that focused on the free flowing energy of the belly, in a historical period where Western women aimed to do the exact opposite with their use of the bodice.

In 1893, there was a huge scandal followed by incredible success.

One important event in the expansion of belly dancing was presented at the Midway Plaisance, at Chicago's World Fair in 1893. A huge scandal was followed by incredible success. Waves of spectators lined up to see the shows. The most famous dancer, Fatima, or "Little Egypt," became a legend, and the dance then spread under the name "Hootchy-Kootchy."

Vignette of the Chicago Fair from the World Fair Puck, 1893, which shows how the Turkish director first advertised the show as a Moral Show, but after failing to sell many tickets, changed it to: Life in the harem. Dream of the Orient. Oriental Dance. The Sultan's Diversion.

A Liberating Distortion

The manager, Sol Bloom, sometimes sat down at the piano to accompany the dancers when they needed a musician. He also created a real mess, which turned out to be a best-selling hit at the fair, along with the improbable Orient and its camels, Bedouins, and mules. The belly dancing presented at the fair as "the harem dance," or "the sultan's diversion," was a distortion for the most part. Nevertheless, this was how the East entered into Western imagination, deeply revolutionizing the perception of the body, and also helping spread the fashion of the Orient. The images offered an exotic place rich with women, fantasy and sensuality. [2]

At this time, belly dancing was not exactly recognized as "art." The same "Little Egypt" had to protest about how her name was being used in some of the shows. They claimed the shows were inspired by her dance, but in reality it was more of an erotic dance without much art that attracted a mostly male audience. The belly dancing was, however, a liberating and therapeutic event, and was important for western society during a period of delicate transition, as it came out of the puritan Victorian era. The body had a revolution and this dance was one of the instruments used in its liberation. Woman asked for the right to vote, and at the same time, the sensual flavor of belly dancing was helping them reclaim their bodies with a more natural and fluid presence.[3]

It was the beginning of women's emancipation in a society that was permeated with rigidity. As a result, the anxiety provoked by such an exuberant dance produced a contradictory female model: the femme fatale. She was a temptress, a sensual, dangerous viper brought to life in the theater with the character Salome. This fueled many distortions about the intent of belly

Dancer, choreographer, and pioneer of modern dance in America, Ruth St. Denis took inspiration from the East for the themes and costumes of her dances.

dancing, and the origins of the veiled dance, as we will see in the chapter dedicated to the symbol of the veil. However, belly dancing also contributed to a revealing, artistic movement that then established itself in the United States: modern dance. With its innovative and participatory force, this type of dancing came to propose a new vision of body movement, and its pioneers, Loie Fuller, Ruth St. Denis, and Isadora Duncan, repeatedly took their inspiration from the Orient. When belly dancing was introduced to the Western world with all of its sensationalism, it was not always perceived or followed as "art." However, it served as a cultural catalyst at the end of the 19th century, and with a gradual metamorphosis over the entire 20th century, it found a new use for its own artistic language. From the distortions presented at the world fairs, to the decisive influence on modern dance, belly dancing has recreated itself over and over again. In a creative intertwining of Eastern and Western artists, the dance feeds upon positive innovation. Even today it breaks the social rules and through its thousands of movements, it offers every artist the opportunity to feel, love, and communicate through her body, starting at the core.

But let's go in order. Now we'll take a look at another name: Oriental dance.

Which Orient for "Oriental" dance?

At this point it wouldn't be an Oriental dance anymore, just a Western invention of a dance that re-configures the Orient, based on the model of an Eastern woman who is ready and willing, but has no true life in her.

Understandably, the difficulty our culture has with femininity as it relates to the belly (even in ways that we aren't aware of) forces us to look for other names that would give more value to the experience that belly dancing offers us. Now I'll take it upon myself to discuss the other name commonly used as an alternative to belly dancing: "Oriental dance," or "Oriental belly dance." Presenting itself as a geographical name, it could neutralize the exaggerated, erotic body energy or the uncomfortable associations made with the belly. But what connotations are provoked by the name "Oriental dance?" When I call belly dancing "Oriental dancing," or in French, "danse orientale," I can draw from the ancient Eastern philosophies that try to give back to the experience, the instinct, the spiritual bond with nature and the body. "Orient" also has an origin that is very interesting for our dance, because it comes from the Latin orios, which means "to be born" (where the sun is born). This perception of Oriental dance as the dance of birth, which we will see later on, is very appropriate. It brings us back to the roots of belly dancing, when it was part of the cult of the Mother Goddess. She was also called the "Woman of the Oriental Gateway," because it was said that she had the ability to aid in birth an the continuity of life.

From this point of view, belly dancing can be seen as the original dance, since it definitely came into existence in prehistoric times, before the appearance of the river civilizations. It originally served as a ritual not only for birth, but also conception. In my opinion, though, the name "Oriental dance" causes various problems: it's not very specific, so it could be confused with Japanese or Chinese dance, or any dance found in the vast Orient.

Most importantly, I don't use it because it is still a geographic name that doesn't relate to the dance's essential instrument- the body. It seems that the purpose of this name was to get away from associations with the body for reasons of modesty, or to avoid the stereotypes connected to the belly, which I talked about previously. I get the impression that by using a geographical name, people are trying to neutralize the prejudices linked to the belly and its erotic power, and so the name has been transferred from the reference point of the female anatomy to a geographical one: the Orient.

But by calling belly dancing "Oriental," are we really avoiding the heavy prejudices and neutralizing the erotic suggestions? Or, as I think might be the case, is the name "Oriental dance" just a byproduct of the exotic Orient and of the even more erotic harem (prohibited place).

A good part of the Eastern imagery, which still dominates belly dancing performances, profits from the ideas that originated under Western colonial law. In particular, those that lead to the stereotypes about the "lustful and apparently uninhibited" Oriental sensuality.[5] These ideas were associated with the harem, and the sultans with their naked concubines laying about, which inspired the collective fantasies about belly dancing and gave it an arousing and exotic reputation.

> *This kind of erotic depiction was invented by Western painters who had never traveled to the Middle East, but imagined the harem to be a place with lustful women and naked dancers. It was not considered to be just a fantasy, but a realistic representation, and it spread the vision of belly dancing as a provocative harem dance. The Odalisques of Ingres.* The Turkish Baths, *1862, Paris, Louvre.*

At this point it wouldn't be an Oriental dance anymore, just a Western invention of a dance that reconfigures the Orient, based on the model of an Eastern woman who is ready and willing, but has no true life in her. It seems to me that the name "Oriental dance" favors the Western distortions regarding the Orient, labeling it as "the harem dance." According to the misconceptions, the harem was an atmosphere of erotic fantasies where we still mistakenly believe today that belly dancing was invented, but we'll get to that later.

Another name commonly used for belly dancing, "*raks-sharki*," is implemented today in order to provide a touch of respectability or cultural credibility to the dance. With the term *raks-sharki*, one sometimes tries to indicate the "most authentic" or "best" style of belly dancing. However, unless it is only used by belly dancers, this name should be translated for the people who don't know Arabic. Then arises the problem that *raks-sharki* literally means "Oriental dance," a term that can create confusion, as I said before.

For the most part, raks-sharki refers to an Egyptian style of belly dancing that has been influenced by Classical dance, and is very beautiful, elaborate, and refined. But before you choose this name, I would like to point out that we shouldn't exclude or discredit the other styles and interpretations that equally belong to the big family of belly dancing, and that are important to our art. For example, the Turkish style, not very well known, but well interpreted, is very attractive when performed by professional dancers. Its movements are energetic and spontaneous; there are some figures lying on the ground, which is not illegal there as in Egypt, and it is more closely connected to the Romanies (gypsy population) than the Egyptian style is. It is less refined, but very articulate and free, and it too merits a part in the artistic heritage of belly dancing. For this reason, I wouldn't want to use a name that suggests there is only one "correct or pure" way to interpret it.

Belly dancing is by nature a mixed breed. There are various styles and interpretations, and these different artistic choices should not only be tolerated, but welcomed and respected as valid. So, let's try "Middle Eastern dance," which is the right name if we want to assign a location to belly dancing, *as well as* the other folkloristic dances of the Middle Eastern countries.

Belly dancing is by nature a mixed breed. There are various styles and interpretations.

Few people know this, but belly dancing plays a part in the popular folklore of different Middle Eastern countries, and it is known by different names: in Greece, *cifta telli* (which was the same name given to the dance that honored the Goddess Aphrodite)[6]; in Turkey, *rakkase*, and in Egypt, *raks-sharki* (the more elaborate style of professional dancers), but also *raks-baladi* (the dance of the people). [7]

Personally, I greatly appreciate and admire the artistic development that belly dancing has had in the Middle Eastern countries. Whoever wants to understand its depth needs to understand the cultures that have brought it to its peak. But rather than defining it geographically or culturally, I think it is fundamental to look for the unity, and to give relevance to the aspects of the dance that make it an art with *universal significance*, and that restore its importance as a dance that pays homage to the *female principle*, thanks to its language centered on the belly and the land.

This universal language- which makes it attractive to women of different nationalities and cultures- transcends the definition of "folkloric dance" of the Middle Eastern countries, because it draws not only from the "doctrine of the people," as folklore does (*folk*- people, *lore*- doctrine), but from the feminine, which is immanent in every woman.

Art breaks geographical confines and moves towards other countries in a positive way, creating solidarity. Learning a dance that is considered to be Middle Eastern presents an opening for women of the Western world, giving them the opportunity to learn a language that is foreign and exotic, but only in appearance.

> In order to strengthen our awareness, we need to be the ones who seek the art that best fits us as individuals.

In order to strengthen our awareness, we need to be the ones who seek the art that best fits us as individuals, whatever attracts us. It is here that we instinctively wish to go, as if we suspected to find in that exact place, the right thing to dissolve our creative blocks, and the right bridge to get to our inner beings.

Although belly dancing has its own characteristic language, which gives it its identity as a dynamic manifestation, its execution cannot be limited to repeating steps and choreography. It wouldn't be essential for us as women if there weren't a personal revelation in every move, every step, every stare. This diversity accounts for its growth through the unique contributions of people who dedicate themselves to it seriously and passionately.

It is encouraging to see how cultural diversity alone can enrich the artistic language, what we have to say- *the content of our dance*- and how we say it- *our gestures*.

This discovery has to do with the actual experience of the feminine that we get through the language of the belly-centered dance. It's something personal and unique because it regards every woman, her story, her experiences, and the sensuality that she expresses in her own way through improvisation.

> The dance is something personal and unique because it regards every woman and her story.

A woman who makes her body sensitive and, opening herself to the experience of this dance, focuses the movements on her belly, travels back in time, to a period where time doesn't exist. Through her dance she verifies a sacred, feminine vision of the world that includes her culture or homeland.

The Vitality of Belly Dancing

Belly dancing is not a "pure" dance. And for this, it is beautiful. A good part of its vitality has been guaranteed by the interlocking of different cultures' contributions. This happened mainly through immigration, as with the nomadic Romany populations during the 11th and 15th centuries. The Romanies were known by different names such as "Egyptians" (in the past, they were thought to have originated in Egypt), "gitani" in Spain, "tzigani" in Hungary, "banjara" in India, "zingari" in Italy, and "gypsies" in England. They originally came from the Punjab region of India, and they crossed Afghanistan and Pakistan by way of the Persian Gulf, then went on to Egypt, Turkey, and Europe, finishing in Spain. To them we owe the credit of having spread belly dancing to the various countries that they passed through, creating a fusion, a hybrid dance, out of the many traditions that already existed locally.

Thanks to their non-conformist nature, which brought them to live on the outskirts of society, the gypsies were less subject to the religious control of the countries they traveled through. To the religious, this type of dancing and sexuality were expressions that should be repressed, but the Romanies were able to preserve their matriarchal culture that revolved around the spirit of Mother Earth, the Pchuvus, which granted them health and good fortune. Their dance still kept some traces of the ancient representation alive, mimicking the activity of giving birth. This, as we'll see later, was a universal dance. The Romanies elaborated on the tradition and transformed it into a show that followed them wherever they moved. During their travels, the dance evolved, absorbing the influence of other cultures, and eventually becoming the mix we know today as "belly dancing."[8]

It's interesting to note that there are some common characteristics among the Romanies' dances as they appear in different countries, such as India, Egypt, Morocco, Turkey, and Spain: the hip movements, the rhythmic beating of feet and hands, the lateral movement of the head and thorax, and the vivaciousness of the hand gestures.

The ghawazee dancers of Egypt are very famous, though their origins are obscure (they may be descendants of the Indo-Persian gypsies), likewise are the cengi dancers of Turkey (cengi no doubt comes from the word cengene, which means gypsy). Even in our day and age, the gypsy neighborhoods in Istanbul and Sulukule, are famous for belly dancing. [9]

Ouled Nail from Nigeria, early 1900's. (photo: Elizabeth Mourat, private collection)

For centuries in the Middle East, the belly dancer's art has been a central part of all the celebrations that manifest spiritual life in the community and of the rites of passage: weddings, baptisms, circumcisions, as well as religious holidays. However, the use of all of these is progressively declining.

Unfortunately in Egypt, where in the past belly dancing had an incredible amount of vitality, it is now rare to see artistic and elaborate belly dancing due to the threats of the fanatic fundamentalists who would like to do away with the dance forever. They persecute professional dancers as enemies of Islam to the point where many have withdrawn from their careers for "religious motives" (they are offered money to stop dancing and to wear the veil).*

The dance is also disappearing in Egypt because of the law passed by Ahmed al-Amaoui, Minister of Labor, which prohibits foreign dancers to work. This is mainly because they have been accused of taking jobs away from the local dancers. However, the situation looks like it may change under the government of Mubarak, who will go back a step by reinstating the foreigners. They're even talking about opening a state academy of dance!

The spread of belly dancing throughout the world guarantees its survival, and therefore, cancels out the risk of it being extinguished in the Middle East for any political, religious, or social reason.

Thanks to the creative, cultural encounter of artists from different countries and backgrounds, the dance can always count on a stimulus of new energy, which will not surrender to the Oriental-based stereotypes of the 19th century, nor to current political issues. In Europe, there is a strong cultural exchange and artists born in the Middle East find it easier to become recognized in professional dance schools and to dedicate themselves to teaching openly. Here they can share their culture, and at the same time, be inspired by the culture that is hosting them.

Belly dancing has inspired people all around the world to make different types of videos, from instructional to spectacular. There are also many research books that can be helpful in understanding belly dancing's roots, its technique, the different styles, and the wisdom that lies behind its movements.

One very interesting application of belly dancing is in the area of maternity. There are prenatal courses that openly use the techniques, inviting future mo-

---

* For more on this theme, readers should look at: *A Trade Like Any Other*, K. Van Nieuwkerk and *Padrone del desiderio*, G. Brooks, see chapter 12. *The New York Times*, Jan. 20, 2004, and *Egitto il ballo del peccato. La Repubblica*, Aug. 20, 2003.

thers not to hide themselves when they are expecting, but instead, to dance with joy and show off their big bellies.

Around the world, belly dancing is also recognized in connection with other types of dance: in "fusion." For example, with the language of Flamenco, in the fusion, zambra mora, which is now experiencing great popularity, or even with Colombian rock and folklore, as in Shakira's pop music which, aside from the fact that it was proposed as a commercial dance, has brought belly dancing to even the most remote corners of the world.

The Colombian singer and dancer, Shakira, at the Festival of San Remo, Italy. She is singing "Whenever, wherever," the song that brought belly dancing to the most remote locations

The intertwining is obvious, even when we look at the costumes used in the dance. It's a little-known fact that the "typical" two-piece costume used around the world was conjured up in the United States, and that the veiled dance was also developed there as an art unto itself. This one is characterized by a very specific technique and a lot of variety in its execution; for example, there is a dance with more than one veil, and a dance with the circular veil. In San Francisco, the "tribal belly dance" was also invented, which is presented not as a dance to be followed by a soloist, but rather by a group. They wear costumes with ethnic inspiration, not sequined, and different than those of cabaret dancing (two-piece).

With belly dancing's multi-colored flow, all geographic boundaries are broken, and the tradition is enriched. This millennial art doesn't have another past, or another future, if not the positive mixing among people of different cultures and nationalities, who, being able to create the dance's language, and taking inspiration from the eternal forces that feed it, will themselves to offer a personal contribution. In the end, the thing that is most evident to me is belly dancing's marvelous characteristic of being a dance of integration, a dance that with its cyclical nature, embraces diversity.

But where was belly dancing first invented?
Let's start with the most obvious place: the harem. In society's collective imagination, it is there that belly dancing was born.

> ...a dance that with its cyclical nature, embraces diversity.

WORKS CITED IN CHAPTER 1.3

1. K. Nieuwkerk, *A Trade Like Any Other*.
2. E. Holly, *Noble Dreams and Wicked Pleasures. Orientalism in America 1870-1930*.
3. E. Holly, *Noble Dreams and Wicked Pleasures. Orientalism in America 1870-1930*.
4. E. Said, *Orientalismo*.
5. A. Mourat, *A Comparison of Turkish and Egyptian Oriental Dance*.
6. W. Buonaventura, *Il Serpente e la Sfinge*.
7. W. Buonaventura, *Il Serpente e la Sfinge*.
8. W. Buonaventura, *Il Serpente e la Sfinge*.
9. W. Buonaventura, *Il Serpente e la Sfinge*.

1.4

Western fantasy of belly dancing in the harem.

The Secret Dance of the harem

When I worked in Los Angeles, I took some advice from the chameleon and learned that with great ability, one can adapt to the demands of the surrounding environment, moving safely from one habitat to another. It was in this way, cultivating my ability to change colors and roles as a dancer/actress, that I had the fortune of belonging to that small ten percent of professional artists who make a living off their art. Thanks to this versatility, one time I had the chance to dress in fuscia, for the role of a Mexican immigrant faced with various trials in a big city, and another time, in a little black dress, for a presentation of the Argentine tango. Then there was the army green I wore for the role of a Peruvian guerrilla, when I learned how to hold a weapon and fight with precise choreography. I even dressed as Jasmine, sitting on a flying carpet in my sea-green sari, for an airline commercial.

Obviously, my favorite camouflage was when I got to put on my best "classic" belly dancing costume, the blue and gold one handmade by the famous seamstress Madame Abla from Cairo. This outfit accompanied me to Persian and Arabic weddings, Jewish baptisms, and Hollywood parties.

But I didn't wear it in Jim Carrey's harem scene, which was filmed for the show, "In Living Color:" There I was asked to play the part of a concubine, draped completely with a full-coverage black veil, which left only my eyes revealed. It wasn't exactly an ideal part for someone who wanted to be discovered in the world of show-biz, but there was an advantage to going around unnoticed: I could snoop around the set and study how the other actors worked without disturbing anyone; I sat myself down and, without moving, watched the rehearsals. Of course, I didn't feel very comfortable under the veil. With my breath remaining imprisoned under my clothes, added to the heat of the set, I had the sensation that I was suffocating. It was also very difficult to do the everyday things that we take for granted, like bring a forkful of food to my mouth, or drink from a glass without spilling it all over myself, and I won't even tell you how many times I had to spin around and check myself in the bathroom…anyway, in the end I wore this costume very willingly in order to have the pleasure of working with Jim Carrey and to see him belly dance.

Carrey wore a sparkly, silver jumpsuit open down to his bejeweled belly button, which he managed to move with dexterity in his undulating dance. There were about twenty of us women in his harem, all covered with the same dark veils, under which we happily followed along with the Oriental Elvis's inventions. He sang and danced, inspired by Elvis Presley. He was incredibly uninhibited in his movements. It surprised me that he was so prepared in his choreography, with the undulations that he studied during the breaks, and the moments of improvisation that he inserted every now and then. Like when he rolled his eyes to the rhythm of the music, one of his typical shticks, or when he took off the top part of his outfit (maybe because the set was so hot) and began to do the "zagharid," the Arabs' characteristic shout during moments of joy. Obviously he exaggerated it: he stuck his ton-

A place prohibited to indiscreet eyes, the harem in the imagination of artists and writers has reinforced our fantasies of an exotic and fascinating place. It is the framework of Oriental eroticism, with veiled women and the perfumed favorites that waited to be called for a rendezvous with the sultan which, of course, began with the dance.

gue out while continuing to contort himself and bend all about in front of us. His actions, which were funny and intriguing at the same time, made it inevitable that someone would give into temptation- under the anonymity of the veil, one of the girls freed a hand from her costume and grabbed his tongue, cutting off his chant, and creating a lot of confusion. Carrey went along with the joke, which went on from there, and we all enjoyed ourselves. So the director decided to leave the incident in as the chaotic finale of the sketch, where the Elvis-sultan succumbs to the crowd of adoring women.

But what does Carrey have to do with Elvis and belly dancing?

Our "Elvis's" inspiration surely came from a song that dreamed about the harem. It was the same type of harem introduced at the World Fair in Chicago in 1893, which reflected the Western fantasies about what went on inside the walls and behind locked doors. It was about this that the real Elvis Presley (nicknamed "The Pelvis") sang:

«I'm gonna go where the desert sun is, Go where I know the fun is,
Go where the harem girls dance, Go where there's love and romance.
Go East young man, go East young man.
You'll feel like a sheik, so rich and grand,
With dancing girls at your command».

Harum Scarum. 1965. Go East, Young Man

A place prohibited to indiscreet eyes, the harem in the imagination of artists and writers has reinforced our fantasies of an exotic and fascinating place. It is the framework of Oriental eroticism, with veiled women and the perfumed favorites that waited to be called for a rendezvous with the sultan which, of course, began with the dance.

In reality, the harem's belly dance began as a secret art that the women reserved exclusively for their peers. It was their favorite pastime, a game of improvisation and complicity, and for almost all of them, it was the only pleasure left, behind the closed doors of their golden cage.

Since belly dancing was one of the few occasions for sexual expression, it was in the harem environment that it manifested such a strong eroticism. This contrasted to the strict control that the women were subjected to behind the doors (where even a banana was cut into pieces since it was not to be used for any other means besides alimentation). It was only when the dance became a form of entertainment for the male public that it became lustful and lost its art as "the women's dance."

The harem fantasies will continue to feed into the misrepresentation of belly dancing as an erotic dance made only for the pleasure of men. This symbolism of "the harem dance" is evident in many works, from the songs of Elvis to the model character of belly dancing, Shahrazad, which is the Persian name of the young bride who recounts the stories of *A Thousand and One Nights*. In the films of the 1940's, she presents herself voluptuously spread out on pillows, and languidly whispering: "Just call me Shera." By that time the character Shahrazad

For the harem, belly dancing was the favorite pastime, a game of improvisation and complicity, and for almost all of them, it was the only pleasure left, behind the closed doors of their golden cage.

had lost her original gift for narration. "Her intelligence aimed at nurturing men…all she wanted from men was to converse with them, to whisper in the night" In Arabic they say *samar*, which has a suggestive, poetic tone and is "an invitation to fill the gap between the sexes"[1]

But can we propose an interpretation that differs from this sad portrait? I think it depends primarily on us, on how we present the dance: we can succumb to the stereotypes and go along with the harem dance, or we can present it in a different light that requires a certain culture and artistic preparation, and a lot of courage as we begin to hear about and to propose a belly dance that is different from the expectations.

I know that the portrait of belly dancing as "the harem dance" would be very difficult to uproot; it will always be proposed again. It is even riddled with scientific theories.

I know that the portrait of belly dancing as "the harem dance" would be very difficult to uproot; it will always be proposed again and again. It is even riddled with scientific theories. One theory, proposed by the famous ethologist, Desmond Morris, comes to mind. In his book, *Bodywatching: A Field Guide to the Human Species*, he affirms with a "scientific" overtone that the origin of belly dancing comes from the harem because, "the man was usually very fat, completely lacking all athletic gifts and sexually bored, and his young concubines had to straddle him to bring him to climax, and this is how belly dancing became a specialized activity."

This seems to me to be more like the author's fantasy than profound research on the art's origins. Since it really originated as a sacred, ritual dance among women, it is much more ancient than the era of the harem.

I will do whatever I possibly can to trace the origins of an art that takes form in a fleeting moment and leaves few visible traces.

The antiquity of belly dancing will bring us all the way back to speak about the primordial human era.

WORK CITED IN CHAPTER 1.4

1. F. Mernissi, *L'harem e l'Occidente*.

CHAPTER 2

Secret Roots

«There was a time when you weren't a slave, remember it.
You walked alone, full of laughter, you bathed your naked belly.
You say that you've lost all these memories: remember.
You know how to avoid meeting a bear on your path.
You know the fear of winter when you hear the wolves gathering together;
But you can sit for hours at the top of a tree, waiting for morning to come.
You say that there are no words to describe that time, you say that it doesn't exist.
But remember it. Make an effort to remember.
And if you can't, invent it».

M. *Wittig*, Les Guérillères.

"Maria, have you finished the book?" "When does it come out in the stores?" they ask me. One of my dear friends is afraid that, four years after its conception, the book has become "dated." Really, it's only been three years that I've been writing consistently. What I mean by consistently is that, just like with dancing, I have a specific schedule to keep when I sit down at the computer in the morning and work on it, independently of my state of mind.

Dancing and writing require the same creative process, so when I find myself stressed out about finishing my work, I give myself the same advice I give to those who ask me: "How long will it take me to learn this dance?"

"Forget time as you know it and let yourself go with the experience, the creative process. It could be an amusing discovery, where the end doesn't count as much as the revelation of whatever you are doing at the moment. If you're focused on yourself, you are already on your way and, therefore, you will move ahead for sure. To learn something well, you need to be gentle with yourself and with your body. It's like climbing a ladder: you have to take one step at a time. If you try to jump them all at once because you're in a hurry, you run the risk of hurting yourself.

Why do we always have to think about finishing and nothing else? How would it be to think about making love just to have an orgasm?...either you don't get there at all, or you get there, but without as much pleasure..."

If I make this comparison during class, the women laugh, and to tell the truth, I do too, because I can see that they are amused and that they understand my point right away. The point is, as much with love as with dance, that the art lies in the game of discovery.

Getting back to the book, yes, I would like to see it finished. It's like when you're expecting a baby and you can't wait to see its little face (or their little faces, when you're having twins). But the process of writing is nice; it has enriched my dance and my life, and regardless of its publication, I am happy about where it's bringing me. Anyway, I have time. With belly dancing, you have all the millennia that you want.

(Photo: M. G. Sarandrea).

2.1

The Neolithic Era
and Belly Dancing

M To me it is surprising and wonderful that there are reasons to believe that the roots of belly dancing go all the way back to prehistoric rituals, and that its language is signed and woven into the fabric of the feminine experience of the archaic world. But I don't search for dates. It's neither possible, nor auspicious to discuss the dates of belly dancing's origins. Its manifestation belongs to various cultures, that certainly existed in different times and epochs. It could be the oldest dance and could bring us back to prehistory, to the Neolithic age (7000-3500 B.C.) and maybe even further, to the Paleolithic era.

During this time appeared the very first images of divine power, which were exemplified by the figure of the Great Mother, the "Venus" represented by the little statues with fertile bellies, and generous hips and breasts. These statuettes were adored by our ancestors 20,000 years ago. Surely belly dancing's prehistoric roots are connected to humanity's experience of the sacred, to the religion, and to the spiritual life of the community.

Typical statuettes from Paleolithic Europe (from left to right): the very famous Venus of Willendorf, Austria, about 25,000 years old. The Venus of Laussel (with a horn, or possibly the moon in hand, carved into the entrance of a grotto-temple in south France), which is surely the most ancient relief sculpture, and the Venus of Lespugue, about 20,000 years old.

Even if it is plausible that the tradition of belly dancing first took form in the Paleolithic era, it is still impossible for me to resist the temptation of thinking that its first generation language was formed during the Neolithic, a time when the world was full of variety and potential.

The Neolithic era is crucial in the history of mankind, because during this phase, human beings witnessed enormously important changes thanks to the "Neolithic revolution," the invention of agriculture, which, according to the religious historian, Mircea Eliade, "is attributed to women without much difficulty."[1]

Not only was the way of obtaining food revolutionary, but also the ways of living in a society, creating familiar and sexual relationships, and practicing magic to guarantee the cooperation of nature in human toil.

The invention of agriculture permitted humans to *deepen the cyclical quality of life*; in fact, it was through agriculture that the human being "...discovered that the cosmos was a living organism, governed by a rhythm, a cycle in which life is closely and necessarily connected to death, because the seed cannot sprout again if not through its own death"[2]

In that moment, a connection was made between the fertility of woman and the fertility of the land. Humans learned that the vegetated world, with its various phases of development, is identical to the unfolding of human life inside the womb of the mother. For the first time, they spoke about populations that sprang from the belly of the earth and, in fact, the belly appears often in many of these stories. The great Belly Goddess is Mother Earth.

The belly became a symbol of the feminine, which represented the mother, and the land- it wasn't adored as the object itself, like an organ or a body part- but it became a symbol of the sacred mystery of our origin and the fertility that it revealed in its changes: menstruation, pregnancy and childbirth.

The procreative aspect of the belly- it's worth saying, the transformation during the period of gestation that is almost like a dance with its changing movements- was full of spiritual meaning and linked to the cosmic rhythm of the land's fertility and the cyclical procession of the moon.

And here we have to remind ourselves that the moon was the *model for primordial humanity*, because it was in the moon's "life," in its transformations, that the human beings first recognized themselves. Not only because life comes to an end, just as the moon dies when it disappears completely, but also because it regenerates itself with a new moon, validating the human hope of regeneration.[3] The moon and its different phases revealed to man that life regenerates itself, it repeats itself rhythmically and doesn't end with death. In the human beings' heavy dependence on a cyclical life, on the phases of agriculture and the moon, we can discover other significant ideas, such as regeneration, eternal youth, salvation, rebirth, and immortality. Ideas in embryonic form that later made up the essential framework of all of the successive religions.[4]

In the new agrarian economy, the Pregnant Goddess of the Paleolithic era transforms into the Goddess of the Land's Fertility. The fertility of humans and animals, the abundance of new sprouts, the flowering of plants, and the processes of growth and weight gain acquired a great deal of importance.[5]

Agriculture transformed human relationships, focusing them on the feminine, the land, and the woman. The woman was, therefore, given power even on an economic level, thanks to her mystic solidarity with the land. She was the one to guarantee fertility and therefore life, and this gave her an enormous religious importance. Her body was seen for its religious character, and her sexuality, fertility, and magic, along with the magic of the land, came into play as religious forces. The woman was the Goddess and her organs were compared to different cosmic phenomena: the woman to Mother Earth, her hair to the grass that provided sustenance, her belly button to the center of the earth, her intestines to labyrinths, her spine to the center of the earth or *axis mundi*, the moon to cosmic change, and finally the belly was compared to a grotto, and was the sacred place of excellence, linked to the origin of all life.[6]

The belly became a symbol of the feminine, which represented the mother, and the land.

The moon was the *model for primordial humanity*, because it was in the moon's "life," in its transformations, that the human beings first recognized themselves.

The Neolithic Era and Belly Dancing

Women at work in the fields. Picture found in the Sahara dessert, North Africa, around 2,000 B.C.

In the Neolithic period, more than 10,000 years ago, the cyclical language of belly dancing was probably first formed. As a ritual dance, it aimed at sanctifying biological life and the cosmic rhythm of transformation that our predecessors felt was anchored in the woman's belly. It is not unlikely that under the form of the dance of life, the sprouting of plants was also mimicked, because fertility and birth were subjects pertinent to women, and surely the analogy that exists between germination and birth arrived in a spontaneous way during a dance.

In this idea of circularity, of spiritual transformation, of life-death-life, that we see in the Neolithic era, the archaic and lunar heritage of belly dancing is enclosed. This is its original heritage. And although we have lost, for the most part, this sacred, nocturnal value of the ancient religions, in favor of the rational, solar aspects of the religions that followed, we cannot avoid being inserted into the natural motion of the moon, the life-death-life that fascinated human beings at the dawning of civilization. It's the same natural motion that has permitted belly dancing to survive for millennia. More than looking for an exact historic or prehistoric reference point for belly dancing, I think it's important to take note of the wonderful *human need* that has made sure that the dance's lunar, primordial, Neolithic message was sent all the way down to our present day. Belly dancing succeeds in speaking to every woman today, as if it were created for her and her time. And so, it is a living, necessary art of the present. When I look away from the differences that exist in the various styles and interpretations of this dance, I gladly feel something that unifies us, something *permanent*, that gives us common ground, that has enchanted and will continue to enchant women and men for generations to come.

I think what makes me passionate about this dance is its original metaphor, its symbolism of transformation, of woman as earth, of woman as the *messenger of life*, as when it inspired the first dances.

> Belly dancing succeeds in speaking to every woman today, as if it were created for her and her time.

WORKS CITED IN CHAPTER 2.1

1. M. Eliade, *Trattato di storia delle religioni.*
2. M. Eliade, *La prova del labirinto.*
3. M. Eliade, *Il sacro e il profano.*
4. M. Eliade, *Il sacro e il profano.*
5. M. Gimbutas, *Il linguaggio della Dea.*
6. M. Eliade, *Il sacro e il profano.*

2.2

The Eternal Presence

«*A woman is inevitably the history of her belly,*
Of the seeds that were fertilized there, or that weren't fertilized,
Or that stopped being fertilized, and of the unrepeatable moment
when she transformed into a goddess.
A women is the history of little things, banality, everyday tasks,
She is the sum of the unmentioned. A woman is always the history of
many men. A woman is the history of her country, of her people.
And she is the history of her roots and her origin,
Of all the women who were nourished by other women,
Who preceded her until she could be born:
A woman is the history of her blood».

M. Serrano, Antigua, vita mia.

I think the fact that belly dancing is always "fresh" and "new" depends mostly on its language, which has deep roots anchored in the feminine. It has proceeded on as an "eternal presence" throughout generations, and it has a strong link to the unconscious, manifesting itself as our dreams, symbols, and pulsations. As an art with a feminine nature, it responds to our need of deep expression tied to the experience of being women, and every woman renews these terms in her own way.

What we can perceive about the origins of belly dancing, even by using our intuition, is that it belongs to the world of feminine archetypes. I think it's worth saying that the primordial models inspire us and bring us to belly dancing, making it become *the feminine archetype poem*. This wonderful aspect that concerns us is the archaic, spiritual heritage of this art. Jung, who developed the idea of interior images, "archetypes," as he called them in his theories of analytical psychology, referred to them as "images from the collective unconscious," which are common to all people and all historical periods. In fact, he wrote "…a thought exists under the form of primordial images, of symbols that are older than the history of man; symbols that have been impressed since primordial times and that continue to live on and replicate themselves in every generation, constituting the foundation of the human psyche."[1]

But where are the feminine symbols anchored? Where do they begin?
The archetypal feminine symbols were introduced "at the beginning of time," by the Goddesses who were considered to be the first examples for different human activities: making love, giving birth, creating through dance. Their example also inspired some of the more insignificant activities, such as washing up, or combing our hair, which were given sacred value in the archaic conscious. At that time, the dance developed an important role: through it they tried to discover nature's mysteries, to make friends with her, and to "help" her carry out her duties.

As an art with a feminine nature, it responds to our need of deep expression tied to the experience of being women.

Belly dancing has passed through the ancient world and evoked profound emotional responses about who we are and about our femininity. It can arouse sensations that can easily become prejudices and push us to consider other philosophies of life to be profane philosophies taken on by our culture for quite some time now. I invite you to refuse to yield to the temptation of seeing the values of the "first" cultures as "inferior," but instead, to open your heart in order to understand the emotion of belly dancing and to feel the hidden meaning behind the gestures that we see today and that were at one time brought to life by the prehistoric women who personified the feminine aspect of divinity, a refined, timeless knowledge.

Thoughts on the Goddess/es

Even though we take it for granted that God has always been imagined to be "masculine," as he is for the monotheistic religions- which believe God, Buddha, or Allah to be the supreme realty- in reality, *this wasn't always the case*. In the great archaic traditions, the divine, creative power belonged to the Goddess (or Goddesses), the first transpersonal source to become an object of worship and religious fear.

I believe that thinking about the Goddess is important, because it helps us find the hidden paths that complete our image of God, offering us the feminine aspects as well, and therefore, the whole picture. As a consequence, it is hopeful that the image of the Goddess might be a significant model for women, but one that also manages to inspire men, because the traits that are usually considered to be feminine in our culture- delicacy, compassion, generosity- belong to the entire human race, just as the qualities seen as masculine- strength, courage, anger- belong to the complete potential of women as well.

She, the primordial force of nature, the Goddess, is the feminine element that gives life to forms and knows were they come from.

A source of life and abundance, she is time and space, she is the mystery that stands apart from her own being and from pairs of opposites.[2]

She is also the reawakening force that stimulates men to love and plants to bloom. She is transformation. In her body, which is the cosmos, all of the different stages of life (birth, life, death) unite. From this point of view, death is not the end, and likewise, birth is not a beginning. They are phases of transformation.[3] The Goddess is the model for women, her image changes throughout life, assuming different roles along the way, and she holds this image in her lap; it is the real and true compilation of feminine potential. She offers herself as sustenance for the creative process, which is expressed not only through dance, but in the value that we give to

The Goddess is the feminine element that gives life to forms and knows were they come from.

human relationships and the Earth itself, ecology, and their importance to us as individuals. Thinking about the Goddess helps us become more aware of our cyclical nature's complexity and richness, and it also whispers something secret in our ears, as Wittig's verse at the beginning of chapter two says, to *remember*, and if we can't do that, to *invent* our own "herstory."

But which one of the many Goddesses am I talking about? As far as the origins of belly dancing are concerned, I am drawing mostly from the energy of the archaic Goddesses closer to the Neolithic period, and from the "Goddess of a Thousand Names," who didn't possess fixed and limited qualities like the later Greek Goddesses who became "specialized." The exemplar figure Athena was the protector of women and female fertility, the Goddess of dance and agriculture, but became known only as the Goddess of wisdom and war.

Head of the goddess Ishtar: many people attribute belly dancing to her cult, which could still date back to the Neolithic Goddess that preceded her and to whom Ishtar was an heir.

Contrastingly, the archaic Goddesses that preceded her show us a much richer and more complex world: the Babylonian Goddess Ishtar (the heiress to the divine- the Neolithic Queen), to whom many people credit the origin of belly dancing, was the "lady of the land," but also the "lady of the heavens." Under the different names assigned to her, the Great Goddess was the master of the animals and plants, and at the same time, the Goddess of the dead and of the Underworld. She was the belly and the tomb.[4]

She was worshiped first as Inanna, then transformed into Anat and Atargatis in ancient Syria, Ashtoreth and Asarte in Canaan and Israel, Iaset and Isis in Egypt, and Aphrodite in Cyprus. So many different names, but the same qualities and attributes confirm that we are talking about the "Goddess of Infinite Names."

The Debate over the Gold Age

I would like to open an important parenthesis regarding two contradictory lines of thinking about the Goddess that currently exist.

As some authors point out, the preponderance of the worship of the feminine may have had absolutely no reflection on women's condition in real life. It's possible that there is no logical equivalence between the exaltation of woman as an object of veneration, and her position in society.[5] There is a similar situation to-day in India, for example, where the by the exaltation of the feminine elements has been very important for centuries, yet it doesn't reflect women's social position in general. And here we find ourselves in the middle of a heated debate, in which for some, the matriarch didn't guarantee equality for women, while for others, it exalted the feminine in every way, including the artistic, economic, and social aspects. The latter point of view is reinforced by the constant archeological findings at sites like Hassuna, Tell Halaf, Samara, Ubais, and most importantly, Catal Huyuk, the biggest Neolithical site ever found. Here lie the remnants of a tranquil, artistic, matriarchal society founded on the religion of the Goddess. It flourished between 7000 and 5000 B.C., in the location of modern day Turkey, and boasted a wide range of arts and trades, which were very obviously dedicated to the Goddess. The settlement had no defensive structures, and even the Neolithic mythology of the region reinforces the impression of a calm, agrarian lifestyle. There proves to be an absence of weapons, and in the 150 or so paintings discovered, there is not a single scene of violence; instead, they *refute the idea that war is a fundamental demon of human nature.*

Neolithic mythology refutes the idea that war is a fundamental demon of human nature.

Concerning the theme of cultures that revolved around the mother figure, the work of Marija Gimbutas is very interesting. She is the eminent scholar and pioneer of archeo-mythology, a discipline based on archeology, comparative mythology, and folklore. In her book, *The Language of the Goddess*, she examines more than 2000 handmade items from ancient Europe, deciphering the secret symbols of the Great Goddess, Lady of the prehistoric world. Her prospective has provided a concrete base for a new way of thinking about our origins. The mythologist, Joseph Campbell, considers the lexicon of painted signs deciphered by Gimbutas to be "a part of humanity's primordial attempt to understand and live in harmony with the beauty and wonder of creation." A vision that is contrary in every aspect to the manipulated systems that would later prevail. In its relationship with dance, the wisdom of thinking about the Goddess is useful to us as inspiration, independent of whether or not it was really a feminine Gold Age, in which women's social power and position reflected the importance given to them by the cult.

The Goddess is equivalent to the Woman as the "feminine essence," that which we share with other women when we dance together. In the different symbols we find poetic inspiration that brings us closer to founts of imagination and to a sacred perception of the world. In this shared dance, the most profound truth is brought to life by the timeless woman that exists in each one of us.

The Goddess is Rhythm

«The Goddess leads us into the spiral dance of life.
She sends forth the winds, the whirling energies
that bind existence in eternal motion.
Through dance, She teaches her children movement and change».

Merlin Stone (cited by I. Stewart in *Sacred Woman, Sacred Dance*).

Luna. Edward Jones.
The Mass Gallery,
London.

The Goddess is rhythm, movement, the cyclical dance that celebrates Life and the transformations of the woman's body, which fall into harmony with those of nature and are regulated by a rhythm, just as dance is. The inborn rhythm of nature itself is expressed in the alternation of day and night, in the seasons that are in harmony with the movement of the sun and earth, in the phases of the moon, in the ebb and flow of the tides that are linked to the moon, in the hibernation periods of animals. The body itself also lives with rhythm, in periods of sleep and wake, effort and rest, in the cyclical unwinding of its functions, such as the alternation of inhaling and exhaling, the circulation of blood, the beating of the heart, the rhythm of menstruation, which assigns the woman to a circular time, change, and the transformation of the body during pregnancy.

Dance helps us get in synch with the body's interior rhythm, and with Life. For us dancers, it's important to be familiar with the rhythm inside of us and to notice that *the music doesn't create the rhythm, but rather invokes our own internal rhythm*. While you dance, you can follow the cadence of your breathing (for example, with the flute music), or follow the percussive rhythm of the music as it corresponds to the beating of your heart, your "visceral percussionist," that keeps the beat for you as long as you live, and evokes the mystic dance of Life: the mother's heart, which the fetus can feel in the belly even before coming into the world.
In ancient civilization, the rhythm of nature had a sacred quality. For example, in the ancient civilization Sumera d'Uruk, the cyclical energy of the seasons and

the year was recognized and preserved in the rituals of that time, and so, one of the main goals of the rituals in the temple of the Goddess Inanna was to "synchronize" one's own rhythm with the rhythm of nature through the sacred dance. This was accompanied by drums and flutes, which are known to be the first musical instruments created by man, and both are still used in belly dancing today. In the Pirenei region of Isturitz, the first flute was found- almost in one piece- carved out of a vulture bone, dating back to about 25,000 years ago.[6]

The first generation belly dancing was based on a way of life that actively participated in the recurring processes of the belly and the earth, and it completely trusted in the rhythm of Life, to which we belong: birth, life, death, and rebirth. The Goddess herself was a dancer who expressed the rhythmic flow of life through her dance, and in this, the eternity of the soul.

The fluttering Eurinome, the oldest Greek goddess, dances and creates the serpent Ophione out of the lofty wind. Then the two join together and give origin to the universe. They say that Aurora, the Goddess of the dawn, had her own places to dance. The Indian Goddess Kali, flutters in a fascinating dance of death that perpetually transforms life, and Oya, according to a song of the Goddess Yoruba, moves her body in a great dance. Legend has it that the Greek Artemis danced at every birth. She was the Goddess of the wilderness, protector of women in labor, the one that the Greek mothers invoked when their labor pains began, finding comfort in

Dance helps us get in synch with the body's interior rhythm, and with Life.

Dance expresses cosmic rhythm, circular time that unwinds with the changing of the seasons. The dance of Human Life. Nicolas Poussin. London, Wallace collection.

the belief that she assisted them during labor. Perhaps this explains the Greek saying, "Where hasn't Artemis danced?"

In Egypt, they tell the story of how Isis (Au Set, Iaset) introduced dance and music to the Egyptian people, and invented the *sistrum* (sacred musical instrument that represents the creative feminine spirit).[7]

There were also other dancing Goddesses in Egypt. For more than 3000 years, Hathor the moon Goddess was the protector of bodily pleasures, and it was said to be here that the soul lies. She was the Lady of dance, music, and touch, and her dance also recalled the Goddess Bast or Bastet, as a symbol of joy.[8]

The Babylonians formed a cult through their dancing in honor of the Goddess Ishtar, which many people place at the origin of belly dancing, while the Sumerians danced to Inanna, the "Queen of the Sky," and the Canaanites celebrated Astarte, the "Goddess of the Uterus," long before the Christian theologians changed her name to "shame."

Very often, the Goddess was represented playing the drums, which was a sacred activity, just like dancing. It aimed at creating a connection with the divine, the beat of the heart, and the belly of the Cosmic Mother. The ritual form of belly dancing celebrated her generative powers, because she was "The One who Gave Life," "The One who Bore Children," and she always reigned as "The Lady of Birth."

WORKS CITED IN CHAPTER 2.2

1. C.G. Jung, *Modern man in search of a soul.*
2. J. Campbell, *Il potere del mito.*
3. S. Husain, *La Dea.*
4. S. Di Lorenzo, *La donna e la sua ombra.*
5. M. Warner, *Sola fra le donne.*
6. J. Clottes, *La preistoria spiegata ai miei nipoti.*
7. L. Redmond, *When The Drummers Where Women.*
8. I. Lexova, *Ancient Egyptian Dances.*

Tomb painting of musicians and dancers in Egyptian rituals that praise nature. Among the musicians, who present a rarely seen frontal view of the body, one is playing the flute and the others are either accompanying the dancers by clapping to the music, or applauding for them. Metropolitan Museum.

The Eternal Presence

2.3

Belly Dancing and Pregnancy

The Dance of Birth

While I was writing about belly dancing's different primitive symbols, I realized that the theme of birth pops out in every one, usually in a random and spontaneous way. This coincidence seemed curious and suggestive to me, and it helped me understand that *it's not possible to talk about the origins of belly dancing without talking about birth*. It's a theme that I have constantly found in the symbols that are connected to belly dancing and rooted in its philosophy. Because, regardless of whether or not we are mothers ourselves, the arrival of every human being on earth is signaled by birth. Birth concerns the Mother as a fundamental archetype. From Her, emanate the feminine symbols that color our dance and that are pertinent to transformation and rebirth, important to a deeper awareness of ourselves.

Behind the "Fertility Venuses," the statuettes representing a calm and generous spirit, hides the beginnings our human awareness of the spiritual dimension of Birth. In these magnificent works of art, the dominant symbolism is the fullness of the belly and breasts, which are often gigantic, and which represent the Goddess as the "Lady of Birth and Pregnancy."

The Goddess Astarte (for the Phoenicians) Ishtar (for the Babylonians) or Inanna (for the Sumerians)- left- who became Aphrodite for the Greeks shortly thereafter. Statuette in alabaster from the 3rd century B.C. Paris, Louvre. The Mycenaean Goddess between two wild goats, ivory, c. 14th century B.C, Ugarit- right.

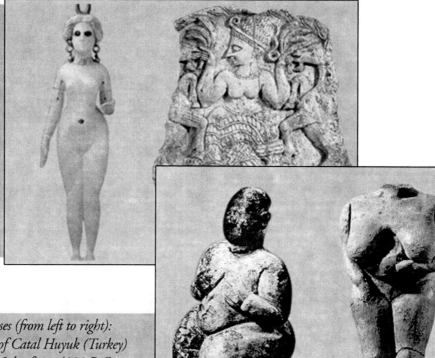

Neolithic Goddesses (from left to right): Mother Goddess of Catal Huyuk (Turkey) and Goddess of Malta from 4000 B.C.

Belly Dancing and Pregnancy

Belly dancing is a natural part of pregnancy; Maria at the Omphalos Theater, during her sixth month of pregnancy with the twins (photo: P. Palmisano).

In ancient times, the mystery of childbirth and the discovery that woman was the creator in the plan of life probably gave place to secret societies and to the first religious rituals in the caverns, uteri of the land, which served the purpose of helping and protecting the woman as she gave birth. Sometimes these rituals constituted real, true mysteries in which the dance played an essential part. Childbirth, as a "primordial event" was surrounded by numerous rites that helped facilitate the process, to relieve pain, and to ward off countless dangers. The time kept by our bodies during childbirth is rhythmic and cyclical, just as in a dance when the powerful symbols of the belly, the breast, the blood, the serpent, and the circle all fuse together. We'll see these symbols as they relate to belly dancing later on.

The metaphor of the woman as "Dispenser of Life and Birth," has been represented through dance all over the world. This is demonstrated by the fact that even today we find feminine, pelvic dancing disguised in different forms: in Hawaii, it's known as the *hula*; the Maori, Polynesian population of New Zealand, dance the *ohelo*, which is a birthing dance done laying down; in the Sudan, the dance of the *Virgin Dinka* uses the stomach muscles in a form of belly dance; the Pygmies in Uganda move their hips in a dance that recalls sexuality and birth; in Cambodia there is a dance with undulations similar to belly dancing; and in Spain, particularly in Andalusia, the Gitani practice the zambra mora, a hybrid of flamenco and belly dancing that is called "the serpent," not without reason.[1]

Belly dancing is still used today by Saudi Arabian women, as a ritual of child birth. They gather together in a circle to accompany the woman in labor, moving their hips and vocally imitating her groans to help her carry out the task of giving birth.[2] The universal nature of birth dances and the various similarities in their movements demonstrate that they are all expressions of the same archetype of Life, which unites the feminine spirit with its cyclical force, and is unequivocally expressed through belly dancing.

Belly dancing is still used today by Saudi Arabian women, as a ritual of childbirth.

The Dance of Reproduction

Belly dancing can still help women who want to have a baby open themselves to the experience of motherhood.

It is very likely that belly dancing was originally intertwined with conception. Researching the different original aspects of the dance, I am fascinated by the image of primordial belly dancing as a Dance of Procreation, even before it was considered to be a Dance of Birth, because it not only helped assist a birth, but also aided in conception.

An important key to understanding this tie, lies in the sacred significance of menstrual blood which, along with the creative aspect of the belly, served the purpose of facilitating the conception of a new life. It's interesting to see how today (even if for different reasons) belly dancing can still help women who want to have a baby open themselves both physically and mentally to the experience of motherhood. They are able to overcome many psychological obstacles that could otherwise sabotage conception if the receptiveness of the body were closed. A lack of receptiveness or psychological well-being could cause just as many problems as the purely physical impediments, and in any case, our mental and physical health are related.

The Life Blood

« The mukula is the tree of menstrual blood,
Of childbirth, of maternal blood.
The history of maternal blood: we believe
That the primordial ancestor gave life
to the grandmother, that the grandmother gave birth to our mother
And that our mother gave us life,
She has doubtless blood:
Without an ancestor, how would we have become visible?
She is the only one who has true blood in every sense of the word».
Hymn of the African Ndebu.

I think it's worthwhile to take a look at the symbolism of menstrual blood in regards to belly dancing and conception, because according to ancient thought, this was the "Envelope of the Soul," and therefore had a very different significance than it does for us today.

Usually, when we speak about menstruation, we pay particular attention to the discomfort that it causes. We use ambiguous names like "that time of the month," or "the red tide," and we whisper about it as if it were something very private or shameful that should be hidden. I think this behavior is due to a heavy dose of reservation, as well as an underlying socio-religious attitude that for centuries, has considered menstruation to be "dirty blood."

Through belly dancing, we can reassign the symbolism of the female body and its functions in a way that is particularly beneficial as far our monthly cycle is concerned.

The positive aspect of this kind of work is evident in the physical, stabilizing benefits that dance has, eliminating common menstrual disturbances, such as amenorrhea (block in menstruation) or dysmenorrhea (pain during menstruation). However, the health benefit that is lesser-known, but of more interest to me, is the metaphorical, lunar, first-generation aspect that unites the body and its functions with its physical, spiritual, and artistic potential.

The religiousness that focused on the mother was a culture of blood, not only because the mother-lineage clan was dominant, but also because it gave menstrual blood an extraordinary value- even if it wasn't always scientifically accurate- as an instrument of the awareness of the cosmos and the rhythm that united it with the transformations of the woman's body.

The experience of menstruation, which literally means "the changing of the moon," signifies an attentive observation of nature, of the rhythms of the cosmos and the body. From this idea, we developed different concepts that are at the base of civilization, such as measure, dimension, meter, incommensurability, that all allowed human beings to become more familiar with the world.

Considered to be the "liquid of Life," menstrual blood represented life itself, because it was not the result of a violent act, but rather sprung forth from rhythm. It went along with the rhythm of the uterus and the moon, and just like the heart, it too had its own cadence in the pulsation of life. The religious aspect of menstrual blood created a strong network with other vital fertility symbols that express the idea of eternity and birth: the snake, which is always shedding its skin, signifies the human aspiration for the unquenchable; the moon, which changes and rises again every month; milk, which is an essential liquid just like blood.

The menstrual blood was thought to be related to the conception of a new life, and there have been many beliefs about conception: the formation of an infant from the mother's ribs (as in the original myth of the Sumerian Goddess Nin-Ti, "Lady of the Rib," and also "Lady of Life," which inspired the later Biblical version of the creation of Eve from Adam's rib bone); conception credited to the light of the moon, and our grandmothers' story of the stork. But the belief most important to belly dancing is that the sacred menstrual blood transformed itself and coagulated to form a baby.

It was believed that the sacred menstrual blood transformed itself and coagulated to form a baby.

In the matriarchal world, it was presumed that no living matter could be developed in the human body without blood, because it was the blood that hosted the soul. Blood was the "first material of existence," the "vehicle of Life," and the "envelope of the soul," and for this it was considered taboo in the sanctified, divine sense.

This primitive notion of blood's prenatal functions made sense to the early humans, because they had not yet recognized the connection between sexual intercourse and pregnancy. The exact duration of pregnancy was unknown to them, so the inability to establish a clear connection between the two things is not as strange as it might seem to us today. A woman could have sex during menopause or before her first menstruation without getting pregnant. It was only the absence of menstrual blood that was a real, evident sign of pregnancy. Therefore, they thought that this cyclical blood was the original sustenance from which a fetus could be formed. And the absence of blood during pregnancy could be explained by its preoccupation with forming the baby inside the body. The idea of menstrual blood being the origin of life still remains today; we might even hear people say that it's a "baby that didn't happen."

For this reason, I don't think I'm crossing the line when I say that the first forms of belly dancing were probably energetic, ritual dances that utilized the rhythmic movement of the belly and pelvis to help the lunar-blood coagulate and form a new life.

The hypothesis of belly dancing being a dance of conception is supported by the etymological and sacred aspects of the blood in the archaic world. There are many words that refer to menstruation, signaling the incomprehensible, supernatural, and divine all at the same time. For example, *sacer* in Latin, or the primordial symbols *da* and *dam*, refers to menstruation and the idea of revealing itself, of the sacred becoming visible through the creative powers of the material- the blood.

An interesting piece of evidence in this hypothesis is the primordial syllable *ma-* to which the Sanskrit words *mens* and *mensis* are related. These words are linked to

> The first forms of belly dancing were probably energetic, ritual dances that utilized the rhythmic movement of the belly and pelvis to help the lunar-blood coagulate and form a new life.

Pregnant women dancing together. Fragment of a terra cotta vase. Iraq, 3000 B.C.

menstruation as well as to the completion of a fluid, circular movement- something that draws our attention to the circular movement prevalent in belly dancing.

The intuition of blood's procreative power is present in the Egyptian myth, *Life Blood* about Isis and her belt, which is also one of belly dancing's specific symbols, as we will see later on. The connection is also evident in the Italian word for pregnancy, *gravidanza*, which interestingly enough contains the word *danza*, dance. Without a doubt, the archaic forms of belly dancing commemorated the mythical moment of original creation, the "instant of creation," the repetition of life rising again and again through conception. From this figuration, it seems that the ancient bond between menstruation and belly dancing is making itself known again: the origins of our dance are colored red by the events of female transformation, by the menstrual cycle and childbirth, which originally brought to life the cycle: birth, death, rebirth.

One could claim that during prehistoric times belly dancing's purpose was to call the rhythms of the belly to completion, to materialize the blood in its most sacred manifestation: life. At the beginning it would have been a Propitiatory Conception Dance, then becoming a ritual Dance of Birth.

Dancing during Pregnancy

Many expectant mothers become curious about belly dancing while they are actually pregnant, and they ask if it is advisable, right, enjoyable, or appropriate to attend lessons during that special time they are experiencing. I would like to give them peace of mind, as well as encourage them to try it after the fourth month, as long as the pregnancy is proceeding as normal.

Pregnant woman feel, in a completely natural way, that the subtle movements, slow gyrations, and undulations, are actually easier to do while you are expecting. It seems contradictory, but it's a surprising fact that I have observed while teaching the same movements to many women both pregnant and not.

Pregnancy loosens up the articulations; it dilates, and exercises a bodily calling that cannot be ignored. During the wait, our natural disposition is to have a more intimate connection with our bodies. I must say that it's paradoxical- because with such a big belly this wouldn't seem to be the case- but it's true that pregnant women have a real privilege during this time when they can truly feel belly dancing and understand its message. Really, belly dancing is supposed to be a celebration of feminine procreativity. It strengthens the silent dialogue bet-

I am the poet of the woman the same as the man,
And I say it is great to be a woman as to be a man,
And I say there is nothing greater than the mother of men.
Walt Whitman, Blades of Grass.
(photo: P. Palmisano).

ween the mother and the baby that is growing inside the private harbor of her belly. With her oscillating movements, she can gently rock her baby.

For those who are familiar with belly dancing's moves, and who have felt the belly's contractions during labor, it is easy to find similarities between the rhythmic contracting and relaxing of the whole abdominal zone, and the undulations, vibrations, etc. that are used in the dance. In fact, I often hear the women in my childbirth preparation classes express that for them, belly dancing is the "gestation dance," as if it were a natural part of the experience. It's a unique sensation that I too have been able to observe during my two pregnancies, one of which was with twins.

The movements of the dance help future mothers concentrate their attention on the belly's creative potential, and to internalize the experience of waiting. The latter task is very helpful during the stages of transformation, because usually women end up focusing their energy on external actions in preparation for the baby's arrival, for example, getting the room ready, buying the stroller, the clothes, and all the necessities, and going to the doctor for sonograms to make sure everything is going alright. These are all very important things that help us prepare for the event, but at times, they can pull us completely away from our center, especially during the third trimester, and they keep us from taking time for ourselves, to dedicate to the body, and to the internal gaze directed at the baby, *who is already there*, and whom we can talk to.

Listening to the body's sensations through dance, an expectant mother has the opportunity to take time to get to know her baby, to patiently dream about it, to feel its presence, and to talk to him or her. During these moments of introspection- when the baby is still in the belly- it is already possible to establish a trusting, loving relationship that will continue after the birth.

Dancing, paired with slow, deep breathing, helps us pleasantly discover the obstetric wisdom of belly dancing. It allows the future mother to feel every part of her body, in particular, the pelvis, *the baby's cradle*, and the breasts, *the sustenance of life*.

Improvising a dance while thinking about the baby on its way, offers the future mother a space for dialogue and creativity (photo: C. Ferrara)

Dancing helps the future mother feel every part of her body, in particular, the pelvis, the baby's cradle, and the breasts, the sustenance of life.

The pelvis, which is the area of most interest, both in pregnancy and belly dancing, always manages to amaze us with all of the different movements it can carry out. Some of these movements are very befitting of childbirth, so much that many women use rotary motions (circles and double circles), or the *shimmy* done very slowly (an alternating movement with bent knees that involves the hips as well), in combination with deep breathing, to reduce labor pains and facilitate the descent of the baby into the birth canal.

Then there is the aesthetic factor, perhaps of lesser importance, but nevertheless appreciated by mothers, that the extensions and contractions of the abdominal zone with different belly dancing moves help keep the skin elastic and protect it from those feared stretch marks.

Finally, and maybe this is even more important for our physical and spiritual integrity after the baby is born, belly dancing encourages a *caring relationship with the body*. It helps to be kind to ourselves as we go back to taking care of our bodies very gradually and without being judgmental. Even if there are still a few extra pounds, which is normal after pregnancy, your "pooch" is not at all a negative feature when it comes to belly dancing. We can begin working with the abdominals gradually: belly dancing gives us time to reemerge from the experience, looking inside ourselves, and feeling the transformations of the body in a positive way.

Many changes take place during the post-partum period as well, often simultaneously: in the family life, the demands of the baby, at work, in household organization, and in the abilities of our bodies. It can be a rough period, and therefore this should be a time when we don't rush ourselves, when we listen, and nourish our babies and ourselves. It helps to be at ease with the body and to patiently re-familiarize ourselves with it, keeping in mind that we don't lose anything through childbirth; we can discover an immense world of joy.

WORK CITED IN CHAPTER 2.3

I J. Voss, *La luna nera*.

Part Two

CHAPTER 3

Belly Dancing's Fundamental Symbols

1 - The Belly

2 - Omphalos - Navel - Center

3 - The Land

4 - The Circle

5 - The Belt around our Hips

6 - The Spiral's Cyclical Manifestation

7 - The Breast, Sustainer of Life

8 - The Hair

9 - "S" for Secret, "S" for Snake

10 - The Hands

11 - The Cymbals' Dialogue

12 - The Water of Life

13 - The Eyes. The Eloquence of the Stare

14 - The Invisible Dance. The Symbolism of the Veil

15 - Fire

3.1

"The symbol implies something vague, unknown, or hidden for us" C.G. Jung (photo J. Mion)

Dancing the Symbol

Because dancing well is not just being able to follow the choreography, it's allowing the dance that already exists inside of us to take flight in the movement of our bodies and through our sensitivity.

It often happens that when we are ready to begin dancing we find a void in front of us. What do I do? Where do I start? And even if I know where to start, what do I do after that? This is where working with symbols comes in as practical assistance, because when I interpret belly dancing's symbols, I am responding to the question of "what to dance, and why?" The idea that we keep in mind through the process of improvising is to avoid a mechanical execution of steps and movements, and to nurture our imagination instead. It is only in this way that we can express ourselves through this dance's profound language. When I feel relaxed and concentrated, I am open to life. I am ready for whatever happens next, and open to the moment and the vital space of "I don't know what will happen, but I'm present and open to my breathing." This type of approach requires us to be calm, and asks us to concentrate on our breathing, and to listen. Because dancing well is not just being able to follow something that's already choreographed, which we learn through imitation. Dancing well is allowing the dance that already exists inside of us to take flight in the movement of our bodies and through our sensitivity. This dance is begun *not by moving*, but by *staying still and listening to our breathing*.

When we improvise, we choose our own paths; it's important not to begin at random, distracted by external elements such as the music, the audience waiting for us, or even our own expectations that led us to set out on a particular path. It's also important not to be distracted by the nervousness that pushes us to do something. The truth is, when we take our time and have faith in the dance that lives inside us, the body will be inspired to use genuine movements, and will be able to let itself go with the flow, down the chosen path.

This is not an easy thing to do, but the symbols make it possible. It worked like a charm for me, when I first began using belly dancing's images to help resolve my students' difficulties in creating dances on their own. This difficulty was evident both in the women who were just beginning a dance course, as well as the more experienced dancers who came to me with many years of serious study under their belts. It seemed incredible to me that they could complain about "not knowing enough" to improvise, and that they preferred to choreograph their dances, trusting in the most familiar sequences that had already been memorized by heart instead of trusting in the soul's inspiration and whatever that exact moment had to offer. I wanted them to draw from their own experiences and start expressing them with their own style, without leaving out the things that were happening at the moment. If you think about it, it's a luxury to be able to work like this, because in our everyday lives we're conditioned to having to get everything done, and to following rhythms that are not a part of nature or our bodies. But by following the body instead, I wanted to make the women become more familiar with belly dancing's poetic universe. I wanted them to have "surprises," the kind that come out of the blue:

a gift, a discovery, a revelation, an unexpected sensation. Surprises are beautiful; they can make you laugh or cry, and they certainly don't leave you feeling indifferent. The content of our unconscious lives in these surprises, and we can see it when we are open to our breathing and to ourselves. They are the jewels of every art, and we can only hope that they happen to us often. We can only look for them by "playing."

The approach of improvising by using the symbols became a window into the dancers' hearts. It allowed them to look inside themselves and to be able to offer a suggestive dance that comes from within; it turned out to be a very positive thing. Little by little, their movements took on the content and fluid qualities that I wanted to pass along. Their breathing was deeper and their stares were more centered. The dancers understood the dance; they really felt it. They recreated it in their own way and communicated their feelings to other people. They knew what to do.
It was then that I really started to appreciate the method that I had developed, so I continued to enrich it through my research in books, and through the experience of the groups. I noticed how this type of approach had the power to reconnect women through the dance's instinctive, sacred knowledge, and through our inner-listening. It was like a bridge that helped them enter the dance's conscious, which comes from "within:" from the belly, from the center, from the land, and from the unconscious.

> Using the symbols, the dancers understood the dance; they really felt it. They recreated it in their own way and communicated their feelings to other people.

The best way to handle this delicate, difficult discovery is through "a game." In fact, when I improvise, I get the sensation that I'm "playing" with the symbols and images. It's the art that comes from the belly, the art of a dance that is truly felt, that sets itself apart from appearances and finds the hidden significance of body movement.

But what is this "game?"
Of course it's the experience of the dance itself that best defines it for us, but now I find myself writing about it, so I will try to describe it in words: I can say that it's the opposite of pre-established order, of memorized choreography that is performed in a mechanical way. It's also the opposite of the voice that inhibits us and tells us to do something, not to move, not to go, not to be curious, not to be silly, not to make ourselves stand out, and to always be rational.
The game is: not being afraid of not knowing, because the body knows.
It's a risk; it's the action of hand that nurtures the imagination; it's the body's spiritual finality; it's the development of our potential; it's a matter of the heart. The game encourages our creativity, *which is the ability to react to everything that happens around us, to choose from the hundreds of possibilities that present themselves to us, and to bring them together to form a response* that has our own individual imprint and is a message full of meaning. Because- and I am completely convinced of this- *everything in belly dancing is secretly intentional.*
There is an eternal language enclosed in it: the "Profound Mother," the wisdom that teaches us to use our bodies as instruments of the soul.[1] The dance externalizes the feminine principle, which is change, transformation and creative spontaneity. And it's not stationary permanence or conventional norms.

The symbols are the center, the heart of imagination. They reveal the secrets of the unconscious and lead us to the origins of the dance. They open our spirit to The All. And for this they are the source of a spirituality anchored in our bodies that promotes life and the development of our art.

> The symbols are a source of a spirituality anchored in our bodies that promotes life and the development of our art.

A characteristic of the symbols is that they ask to be felt, lived, and experienced by the body when we dance, and not just understood rationally. This experience cannot be substituted because the symbols escape rational control and live in our gestures, in the body language that is the dance itself.

So you might ask: why describe the symbols with words in a book? My response to that is: the exploration of reason nourishes our instinct of knowing what to do when we dance. I am trying to stimulate the visual imagination with the symbols that concern us more directly in trying to create a dance in a deeper way. One can't presume to be able to completely describe such a vast subject. I only hope to inspire you to "play" with the dance's images that you find in these lines.

Each symbol can have many different meanings. Usually, when we look at a symbol we realize that the simpler it is, the more meanings it has hidden inside. For example, the circle can represent the moon, the sun, a wheel, a serpent biting its tail, time, the creative source, and so on.

In the end, it's your perception, your exploration of a determined symbol that really counts in the interpretation of belly dancing, which is very personal just as the interpretation of the symbols themselves is.

WORK CITED IN CHAPTER 3.1

1. C. Pinkola Esté, *Donne che corrono coi lupi*.

3 . 2

What I mean
when I say   that belly dancing
is a dance of fertility

To give a general orientation on symbols we can say that in every human population we can find trees, stones, animals, and elements like water and fire, which are all known to carry spiritual messages that go beyond their physical forms, or else they are symbols that express "something more" for the human conscious. This "something more" represents human worries, and the fear itself connected to our primordial needs of survival- such as health, the environment, food resources- but also the human ambitions of security, wealth, power, and spiritual life connected to death, the soul, the future, and eternity. For belly dancing, the themes of fertility and sexuality concern us more directly and since ancient times, they have always been fonts of human interest, just as positive as negative, and full of sacredness.

Here I would like to be careful not to fixate on the idea of belly dancing as a "dance of fertility," so as to make it superficial. I would also like to make it clear that when I speak about this dance's symbols of fertility and fecundity, I intend them to be *symbols of the soul and eternity, centered on the vital source that sustains life through sexuality* (see the symbol of the belt for more on the theme of fertility). I don't refer to belly dancing as an invitation to the sexual act- as it is sometimes reduced to in its execution and observation- a fertility dance that completely precludes the vital-cosmic aspect stemming from the origin. I would like everyone to keep in mind that the symbols express "something more."
When we talk about fertility, birth usually comes to mind, and along with it, death. Really, the symbols of this dance are symbols of life, death, and rebirth. It obviously regards biological birth, but also the mind's creative instruments, which allude to birth as a metaphor to show the descent of the spirit's life and death, and to indicate a spiritual change. This aspect concerns individual discovery and understanding of ourselves, which we put into action through the dance. It indicates a path of growth and, therefore, a new birth.
One very beautiful, unifying characteristic of the symbols is that they transcend geography, race, and time. Because of this we find many dances similar to belly dancing in the most different and the most distant cultures. They all express themselves through similar movements and are anchored in the birth dance of the old race populations. Birth has the idea of rebirth instilled in it; it suggests that there is a life to search for within life itself, a birth that gives meaning to our journey, a rebirth in the profound life of the belly: "We are born to be born," as Neruda told us

What I mean when I say that Belly Dancing is a Dance of Fertility

Are the symbols masculine or feminine?

The symbols have both masculine and feminine values; we can see one gender or the other depending on the message of the literature we use, and the cultural situation, either patriarchal or matriarchal, that we find them in. In this book I look mostly at the symbols' feminine value, which is usually hidden or overlooked, because it is with these that we have a greater need to synchronize ourselves, to enrich the language of belly dancing. However, I don't forget the masculine gender of the symbols because I am convinced that there is a completeness in belly dancing, a balance of two opposites, a union with the other gender, and therefore, a dialogue, a bridge, a fusion (which we can already understand from the music, as I explain in the section "Fire") and for this reason, I included some aspects of the symbols that allude to their masculine potential.

> I am convinced that in belly dancing there is a balance of two opposites, a union with the other gender.

The feminine value, however, remains the inspirational force of this dance, since it was originally at the center of the archaic cult of the Great Goddess, which we talked about earlier. At times, this creative heritage is difficult to manage, because many symbols that exist within belly dancing, were taken from the ancient religions founded on the woman and were then reinterpreted in a patriarchal context, to the detriment of the feminine principle. The fact that many symbols were transformed to have negative meaning over the course of time can influence our interpretation of the dance in an unfavorable way and can weaken its spirit. If we neglect, or fail to look for the ancient symbols that inspired belly dancing, we lose the opportunity to feel their positive values, which are kept alive within the dance, even if they are hidden.

Let's take the example of the serpent, which is an essential symbol for this dance. A long time before it became the symbol of sin in the Garden of Good and Evil, and looked at with repulsion, it was a very powerful, archaic symbol of the female, and it represented the eternal flow of life. If I interpret the serpent keeping in mind only the image that prevails today, I could create a dance that favors the dangerous and threatening aspect, perhaps leading me to fall into the stereotypical interpretation of the *femme fatale*: a modern day Salome. And my dance would leave out many of the other aspects of this symbol full of implications for life.

> In the archaic world, the serpent was a very powerful symbol of the female, and it represented the eternal flow of life.

A more careful reading of belly dancing's content requires us to be in an open mental state, not traditional, and to be receptive to the metaphors suggested by the symbols. They will nourish the imagination and provide answers to the questions: What should I do? Where should I begin? What messages are my gestures hiding? Creating with this kind of awareness, we are led back to our original roots and we are transformed by belly dancing. It becomes the *moving, winding image of the eternal feminine, and it embraces the opposites with its motion, a necessary life transformation.*

3.3

(*Photo: C. Ferrara*).

The Belly

The Belly

My first encounter with belly dancing was a liberating moment, as it is for many women who become passionate about the art. It was as if I took back my own body and femininity through a new center of reference. Dancing with a revealed belly, I learned to look at my body and its round form with pleasure. I felt how wonderful it is to breath deeply, involving your whole belly and melting into the movements of the dance's wave. Later, during my pregnancies, I appreciated more than suffered for the transformation of my body, which changed constantly and required me to adapt and move differently. I learned to dance, to teach, and to live, all starting with my belly, which has its own music, its own cyclical language. I think that a big part of my road toward a good childbirth and a good relationship with creativity and life, is owed to the practice of belly dancing. It taught me to live in my body without locking anything up, but always being open. And this involves well-centered breathing, and the expansion and contraction of the belly, which is the area of the body where movements are first initiated and where they are later called to come back. In a way, this mobility also taught me to be more flexible in my life, and to accept opposing factors, the ups and downs, the natural movement of things and human situations.

It prepared me to experience positively the changes that each phase of life brings along, because over time, I feel that the dance acquires new depth that comes only with life experience, and I can express this with the belly's creativity.

For this reason, I had no problem referring to this dance as "belly dancing." For me, it is the right name and the clearest name. It could be seen as a given, since "belly dancing" is the most common name; however, I arrived at this conclusion after nurturing my curiosity in a long journey of growth and reflection. I realized how a name so loaded with meanings, both positive and negative, which often appear in myths and the collective imagination, could have such power in its sacred symbols that it pushes our attention away as much as it attracts it. I believe that this name of belly dancing, a contradictory name in that it is loved and refused at the same time, is a significant coincidence. We find enclosed in it the invitation to cultivate our gut instinct, our creative capacity. It forces us to look away from appearances and more at the hidden meaning of things. But above all, it is a name that challenges the stereotypes tied to our bodies. It's not a small thing that belly dancing has to offer, this poetic openness to body language, and to the language of the belly in particular.

But how do we root ourselves in the belly while we dance?

Usually, during the lessons, I ask the women to place one hand on the belly as they follow the movements. I watch how it goes, and encourage them, because for many people this action can turn out to be difficult, if not embarrassing. When we go on to the more articulate moves, I ask them to put one hand on the chest and one on the belly to feel how these two zones are connected in the dance and how they "play"

The dance taught me to experience positively the changes that each phase of life brings along.

together. I suggest that they also accompany the body with a stare, focusing their eyes on the hips (not just in the mirror!) and we always work on breathing, which should involve the belly all the way down to the genital region, and not just the chest.

I help them feel the belly "alive" making them try little vibrations with their exhalation (like when you blow your nose and the belly goes in, but a little faster and with rhythm). I also encourage them to dress in a way that accentuates the center of the body, however they want, and so forth.

My goal is not to get them to roll quarters on their bellies, or balance a glass on top and use the abdominal muscles to move it; my intent is to help them act from the inside, to find a feminine, spiritual dimension within the body itself, and to be able to shift their attention from the head to the belly area, little by little, to put themselves in contact with their own creativity, which is intimately related to the womb's secrets.

You know there is a good physical rooting in the belly when you feel the movements that come from it, like a magnetic point. Even the movements that don't appear that they should start there (like when we raise an arm) originate in the belly, and it seems that the energy used to feed all these movements comes from there. This is hard!

Because to get to this kind of centeredness we have to abandon the "on command" control of the body and of situations, and we have to trust in life and in the language of the belly, which develop in cyclical time.

This cyclical time is, therefore, a time that repeats itself, and it is referred to in the symbolic heritage present in the gestures of our dance. But it is inspired by the music as well. In the melodic pieces, it repeats itself, and for many people, it's monotonous and almost intolerably slow.

In fact, we are so accustomed to changing from one thing to another, to speeding up the processes and transformations in life, it's easy to understand why we often feel obligated to construct our dances with many different steps, accents, turns, and variations in direction to try to "control" time and make it less monotonous and more diverse for ourselves as well as the people watching us.

I, on the other hand, like to cultivate the mystery of belly dancing, following the choreographic form suggested by its archaic heritage, and the musical beat that tells me to abandon myself to the dance's rhythmic language and to persist in the movements that come to me, which are really suggested by the body itself. One movement brings another one along, "it transforms," and the dance has a magnetic quality, with its gestures that almost seem to be suspended in mid air, and sometimes, they stop completely for a second, as if to stop time.

This liquid, full, suspended dance doesn't contrast with the natural rhythm of our bodies, and it can develop slowly, but it can also be rhythmic and forceful. It completely involves the both the dancer and whoever observes it from the outside, because it is lived "on the inside:" it's sensual and nourished by breathing and emotions. It's a cyclical dance of transformation anchored in the cosmic belly, in the archetype of the Profound Mother.

My intent is to help them act from the inside, to find a feminine, spiritual dimension within the body itself, and to be able to shift their attention from the head to the belly area, little by little, to put themselves in contact with their own creativity, which is intimately related to the secret of womb.

This cyclical effect is expressed in the dance's circular movements that transform from one to another in infinite figures. They have the belly button as their center, and the extremities of the body as their circumference. In the belly button is enclosed the mystery of life itself, and the primordial intuition that the sacredness of life and immortality find themselves in a center.

And now let's go on to discuss the symbolism of the omphalos, the "magnet," the central point of belly dancing.

3.4

Omphalos
Navel - Center

Omphalos

«At the still point of the turning world, neither flesh nor fleshless,
Neither from nor towards; at the still point, there the dance is,
But neither arrest nor movement. And do not call it fixity,
Where past and future are gathered.
Neither movement from nor towards,Neither ascent nor decline.
Except for the point, the still point,
There would be no dance, and there is only the dance».

T.S. Eliot, Four Quartets.

Unfortunately, the idea of the center, or omphalos, nowadays doesn't directly evoke everything that the primordial tradition of belly dancing had in its vision. Many of the values of this symbol as an emblem of the origin have been forgotten or covered up, just as the idea that the belly button is a gift from our origin has become a completely foreign concept to us today. Let's take a look at this symbol as it was intended to be seen in the ancient lunar religions.

The Primordial Omphalos

«...the belly button is the sign that makes us human and not supernatural or immortal: and this is a sign worthy of being loved!».

Joseph Campbell

Being familiar with the symbolism that held the center as an expression of the soul, we can come closer to verifying belly dancing and feeling the omphalos in the original character of the dance: the center of the original Unity's being and image. In prehistoric eras, the *omphalos* concentrated on the essence of the Mother, the center of her body, where time began, where life originated, the point corresponding to the center of the earth, to which life would have returned after death for the specific purpose of being reborn.

The center was seen as both the beginning and the end of all things. The *omphalos* was the main point, without form or dimension. It was invisible, and therefore, the image of primordial Unity.[1]

According to many traditions, the universe originated from a navel and took on a form that radiated out in four directions. As a symbol of vital power that dominates the blind, monstrous forces of chaos, the *omphalos* is the central point in which the dimensions of time and space in the human state are decided upon, the traces of the world's axis, the seat of the mystery of mankind's origin.[2]

The *omphalos* had already been represented in the architecture of Neolithic tombs. It was depicted as a protrusion on the summit of a hill that represented the pregnant belly of the Goddess.[3] Nowadays, many sacred places are still situated on hills, an idea that leaves us to perceive, even in an indirect or subconscious way, the feminine symbolism of the land. We can even speak about the Mediterranean Sea drawing from the symbolism of the navel as, "the belly button of the world," which was the name that inspired the Romans to consider it to be the center of their empire.

One of the oldest representations of the center was the stone called *omphalos*, because the prehistoric human beings saw a divine manifestation in the hardness and immutability of the rock, which contrasted with their own precarious and transitory lives.

> «*The* omphalos *could have been represented by stones in different shapes: a pillar, a menhir, or a cone-shaped stone. This last type was usually white and straight with an egg-shaped top, and in various cases, encircled by one serpent, a symbol of the umbilical cord, or by more serpents, presented as sexual companions, a symbol of the union of the sexes. It was considered to be a "prophetic stone," and thus, a "talking stone," because it gave oracles thanks to the spiritual influence that supported it.*» (R. Guénon).

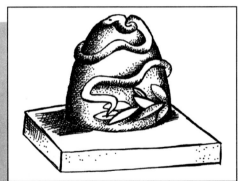

The omphalos is the central point in which the dimensions of time and space in the human state are decided upon, the traces of the world's axis, the seat of the mystery of mankind's origin.

An intriguing feminine symbolism is hidden in the rock, because it was probably the most ancient representation of the Great Mother, just like the Islamic Ka'ba and the *omphalos* of Delphi, the "Temple of the Belly," where Mother Earth was worshipped long before Apollo.

The Fertility Stone

Fertility is a very important attribute of the navel. As the point of prenatal contact between mother and child, it is the original bond through which every living being comes into existence. Thus, it was believed that the sacred stone that represented the navel favored pregnancy.

As a good luck charm for fertility, even today in the Middle East, newlyweds take pictures placing their hands on the belly of a dancer.

The virtue of these stones can be witnessed in the use of them by many different cultures, that all connect them to fertility. For example, in India, newlyweds go to the megaliths to ask for children; infertile women in Salem believe that there are powers that can impregnate them in the dolmen (prehistoric slabs of rock), so they rub themselves against the belly-stones after giving an offering; even the woman of the Maidu tribe in California touch a certain rock that resembles a pregnant woman, when they want to have children themselves. The ancient use of the slide was thought to help in conceiving children; the women slid along a consecrated rock, and newlyweds also went to rub their bellies on the rock during the first few nights of their marriage.

The fertilization stone then became the birth stone, and it was thought that simply touching it would bring the fortune of an easy delivery.[4]

As a good luck charm for fertility, even today in the Middle East, newlyweds take pictures placing their hands on the belly of a dancer.

The Belly Button in Belly Dancing

By using a jewel, a belly button ring, or henna, belly dancers draw attention to a fundamentally erotic area of the body. At the same time, they draw from the ancient symbolism of the navel as "omphalos," center of every human being, and center of the universe, which flaunted a feminine, sacred, and sensual body in the matriarchal tradition.

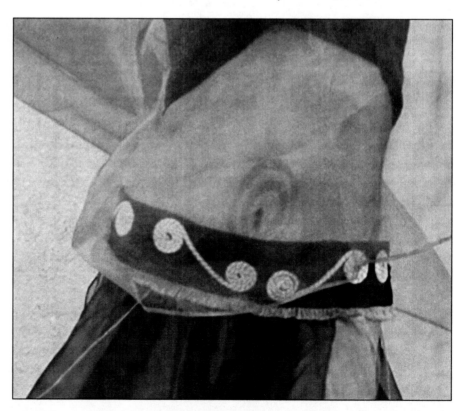

In belly dancing, the navel acts as the center for every step, it radiates its undulating energy through all parts of the body. And the body becomes completely involved in carrying out the movements, primarily circles and spirals.

These shapes, which originate at the belly button and have a cyclical nature that unfolds in two complementary phases: starting from the center, they have a centrifugal spinning movement that radiates energy away from itself, and then eventually completes itself with a centripetal movement that brings the energy back into the center. This dynamic is similar to the vital function of the blood, which starts off from the heart and spreads throughout the organism, giving it life, and then returns to the heart, the vital center. But then, it is also similar to the process of breathing, which acts as an exchange with our surroundings, and helps us understand our deepest sentiments, our fears. With inhalation (centrifugal phase), the belly expands and takes in air and vital energy. With exhalation (centripetal phase), the belly contracts while it empties itself of the air that had filled it before, thus returning to the center of the body.

Enclosed in the symbol of the navel, there is a nice metaphor of the unity of opposites. As much as the "fixed point," the center, represents equilibrium and harmony, it is also the meeting point where the union of male and female is verified, for example, through sexuality and the conception of a new life.

The belly button is a bridge for belly dancing. It is a fixed point that harmonizes and balances the movements that reach upwards with those that focus on the ground; it acts as a pivot

The belly button is the inner threshold. Through a dance focused on breathing concentration, and the belly's expansion, this threshold opens us up to the primordial unity of life.

for the body's different rotations, and as a passageway between the spins that are followed through to the left and then to the right, or vice versa. It unites the movements that are carried out in one place with those that move the body around the space surrounding it. More importantly, it welcomes the concept of life-death-life that is essential to truly understanding the dance.

The belly button is the inner threshold. Through a dance focused on breathing concentration, and the belly's expansion, this threshold opens us up to the primordial unity of life, to an equilibrium in the movement of opposites. It contains an idea that is hard to express in words: eternity.

Belly dancing calls for a transformation and an opening to the deep, sensual spirit of our centers.

WORKS CITED IN CHAPTER 3.6

1. R. Guénon, *Simboli della scienza sacra.*
2. J. Chevalier, A. Gheerbrandt, *Dizionario dei simboli.*
3. M. Gimbutas, *Il linguaggio della Dea.*
4. M. Eliade, *Trattato di storia delle religioni.*

3.5

3 The Land

The Land

«*Tierra, me gustas
En la arcilla y la arena,
te levanto y te formo,
como tù me formaste,
y ruedas de mis dedos
como yo desprendida
voy a volver a tu matriz extensa*».

«*Land, I like you,
In the clay and in the sand,
I lift you up and give you form
Like you gave me form,
And you slip from my fingers
Like I was let loose,
Someday I'll return to your vast
womb.*».

P. Neruda, Odas elementales.

Feeling the land, feeling grounded is important not only because it allows us to do the movements correctly, but also because it is an essential feeling in life.

When I started studying belly dancing in New York, one thing that surprised me during practice was that its movements constantly called me back to the earth. It was not like classical dance, which tries to challenge gravity by elongating the body; on the contrary, it was almost as if the movements and the body were seduced by this force. It allowed me to keep my feet planted on the actual ground, and I wasn't supposed to fight it, I was supposed to go with it.

The body took on big, round shapes; it seemed heavy. It was relaxed but not floppy. The muscles used were only those that served to make a determined movement. The hips didn't run away from the earth, but seeming rotund and soft, they moved closer to it, almost so that I had to sit down.

The very flexible spine, protected by the position of the legs, was free to bend in different ways. There was the bounce, a little vertical flex coming from the knees, which made me feel like I was playing with the force of the ground, and is used in many steps. Then the shimmy, the sensual shaking of the whole body that seemed as if it wanted to drill me into the ground. And finally, there was the dance done kneeling or lying on the ground. I felt that my legs and feet were parallel and strongly anchored to the ground; I discovered how to connect with the ground: the most important thing, the secret, was in the knees, which always stayed a little bent in this dance- with only a few exceptions- even when I felt like I should straighten them completely (when I did lateral accents with my hips or danced half way up on my toes).

What a comfort it was to maintain this friendly support, this embracing of bare feet, in this dance that came and went while the earth offered steady energy. I felt like I was part of a whole, a strong and sensual whole. It was the same sensation of having my feet anchored strongly to the ground that gave me a focal point and helped me when I gave birth to my children. Feeling the land, feeling "grounded" is important for beginners, not only because it allows them to do the movements correctly, but also because it is an essential feeling in life, that puts us in immediate contact with basic realities: with the body, sexuality, and the people we have relationships with.1 Anchoring yourself to the land, in fact, means being in the here and now, without running away from the body or its needs.

For women, the land is also an example to live by, because it has always been an expressive symbol of the feminine. The great traveler and historian Herodotus (5th century B.C, Greece) pointed out that all of the names given to the earth were feminine and that a "Father Earth" never existed:[2] Urd, Erda, Erta, Hretha, Eortha, Nerthus, Erce, Urth, Artha, Edda, Heortha, Gaia, Rea, Ops, Hel, Hera, Demetra. The only exception was the Egyptian god Gebb, but it seems that even this was a case of grammatical nature, because as Eliade explains, the word for sky was feminine, belonging to the Goddess Nut, and the earth belonged to the God Gebb.[3]

The symbol of land has the mysterious significance of being the origin and source of every living thing. She is the one who nurtures all of her terrestrial offspring, and who gave us life. It is to her that we return when we die. "Naked, I came out of my mother's belly, and naked I will return," exclaimed Job as he lay prostrate on the ground, comparing mother earth to the maternal belly (1:21). The earth is the source of strength and fertility.
The ancient use of the word "mud" was positive, due to the fact that the world and human beings were made of it, according to most of the creation stories.4
The Earth is seen as "the belly of humanity" in its characteristic of Mother, and

Almost all of belly dancing's movements are carried out with the knees a little bit bent. The dance's real fluidity is owed to this characteristic, as well as its winding movements (photo: C. Ferrara).

The earth is the source of strength and fertility. The ancient use of the word "mud" was positive, due to the fact that the world and human beings were made of it, according to most of the creation stories.

Childbirth, as it is expressed by the Egyptian hieroglyph.

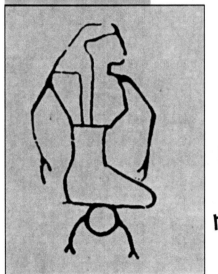

while the Earth is the mother of all mankind, the woman, the maternal belly, is the original Earth of every human being.

This fundamental line of thinking, which is that the human mother is none other than the representative of the Great Mother Earth, is reflected in the rituals of child-bearing, and in the birthing positions based on the ground (the *humi positio*), which are found all over the world. In fact, a woman who is left to her own instinct, looks for a vertical stance when she has to choose the most agreeable position (standing up, kneeling, squatting, sitting). These positions don't exclude the influx of the earth, and they are essential for a smooth delivery, because they go along with the contractions of the uterus and the pushes of the woman giving birth, adding extra pressure.[5]

The ancient Goddesses of birth, Eileithyia, Damia, Auxeia are represented (just as the Goddesses of all the agrarian populations of the world) in a kneeling position, in the exact same position as the woman who gives birth on natural land. The Egyptian hieroglyphic for childbirth also depicts a woman squatting down.

The Real Land that Belly Dancing Belongs to

The land that we are born in has a sacred quality for us, and those of us who have had to leave our land for one reason or another, are especially aware of this fact. For us, it almost becomes a make-believe place and we think of it as we would think of places in children's fairytales.

The land that we are born in has a sacred quality for us, and those of us who have had to leave our land for one reason or another, are especially aware of this fact.

I have here with me a handful of earth that I keep in a baby food jar. It is very red and has a strong scent, and it makes me feel close to my father. It's a primordial sustenance for me: every now and then I go smell its perfume of guayaba fruit and dream about a day when there will be peace in Colombia and I'll be able to go back to my land with my husband and children, without feeling like we are risking our lives.

It's only a handful of land, but it has a great power over me; it reminds me that I am part of the land, and the land is part of me. But maybe it reminds me, more simply, that there is only one land.

One of the most beautiful things that belly dancing has offered me is the chance to travel the world and get to know and exchange points of view with people of different nationalities, races, and religions. The dance brings us together. It creates an attitude of openness to the differences of others and, in a certain way, it softens up even our firmest ideas. For this reason, I feel bad about the arguments that sometimes arise between Arabic and European dancers, about the real land that belly dancing belongs to, as if it absolutely has to take sides and claim one or the other as its own.

The fact that saddens me most of all, is that there is no openness, no feeling of cooperation in this art that is already difficult in other respects, and that the discussions about where we were born and what cultures that we grew up in, only create a bigger barrier between us.

In belly dancing, I see an opportunity to bring the feminine source to life and to celebrate the ethnic, cultural, and spiritual diversity of all the people that participate in it. This point of view also brings along the responsibility of those who dedicate themselves to the dance to learn the language to make it become "my dance." It is the dance of every individual who experiences it with awareness and turns it into something that is not strange and exotic, but a dance that has roots in the body, in the body's memory, and that expresses itself with gestures that are both *characteristic and personalized* at the same time.

Let me give you an example: in my "hybrid dance"- I call it that because I draw from different sources- I use movements from the folklore of different Arabic countries, but I also studied moves that I decided weren't for me, so I don't feel like I should to use them if I want to create an "authentic dance." By the same token, I love to do a nice long dance with a veil, but I don't think that it's wrong that dancers working in Middle Eastern countries don't perform a true veil dance if it doesn't suit their tastes or culture.

In a dance that is spread throughout the world, I think it's important to demand a mutual respect and to leave room for differences and diversity. If it's a good thing for every dancer to develop her own unique, personal style, then it's not a good thing to trap belly dancing into an imaginary geographical area that makes us forget the real meaning of Land.

The "Land," a key element in this dance, doesn't have a purely geographical meaning, with countries and regions divided like the pieces of a puzzle. Belly dancing exists as a dance that celebrates the land that we are all part of.

I don't think that we can separate the respect that we have for ourselves and for the dance that we practice, from the respect that we have for the land. Arts like belly dancing that are inspired by the land, possess a far-away calling, an echo of respect for nature, which we have manipulated to serve our material needs for much too long. The bond with land is common to all humanity; we are her sons and daughters and this ecological line of thinking brings us back to the archaic cultures that lived in harmony with nature.

As a dance focused on the feminine source, belly dancing is the reminder of a time when it was possible to live peacefully on one land (specifically in the

Belly dancing exists as a dance that celebrates the land that we are all part of.

The Land

Middle East), under the serene watch of the Goddess. This was before it was overthrown by the belligerent Gods that succeeded the Goddesses and that still today reclaim the Land for themselves with wars in the name of religion.

> The peaceful, matriarchal organization of our prehistory shows us that war is not one of humanity's natural inheritances, even though it seems like it has always existed since the "beginning of time."

The peaceful, matriarchal organization of our prehistory shows us that war is not one of humanity's natural inheritances, even though it seems like it has always existed since the "beginning of time."

The Goddesses didn't inspire war. Those cultures didn't produce deadly weapons or construct fortifications in inaccessible locations as their successors did , not even when they discovered metal-working. Instead, they built beautiful tomb-sanctuaries and temples, comfortable homes in villages of modest size, and created wonderful ceramics and sculptures. There was, as Gimbutas affirms, a long period of notable creativity and stability, an art culture. [6]

Belly dancing, as an art-symbol of peace and life, recalls the culture of the Great Mother, where cooperation ruled. I think that belly dancing's current popularity expresses a longing for serenity, a calling for Peace.

Will anyone second that?

WORKS CITED IN CHAPTER 3.5

1. A. Lowen, *La spiritualità del corpo.*
2. B. Walker, *The Book of Myths and Secrets.*
3. M. Eliade, *Trattato di storia delle religioni.*
4. C. Pinkola Estés, *Donne che corrono coi lupi.*
5. J. Balaskas, *Manuale del parto attivo.*
6. M. Gimbutas, *Il linguaggio della Dea.*

Circle Formation with the dancers at IALS in Rome (photo: Maristella)

3.6

The 4 Circle

The Circle

Now I'd like to propose an activity: In a seated position, start with the head and work your way down, trying to draw circles with each area of the body. Don't worry if some are more difficult than others, because with a little practice you'll be able to do them all in time. Try to do it so that the movement is fluid and one circle dissolves into the next.

Breathe slowly and at the same time, make soft and continuous circles: start by making a very big circle with your head, keeping your back straight, and letting your hair fall around you. Continue to move like this until you feel relaxed, then follow with the shoulders; push both of them at the same time, backward and forward; try to stretch an arm out and draw circles using one shoulder at a time. Now extend your arms up above your head and open them slowly to the sides. Draw circles with your hands turning them at the wrists, first backward, a typical movement we use in belly dancing, and then forward, a movement typical of the flamenco.

Now, holding your hair back with your hands, try to rotate the rib cage in a circle, starting on one side. This circle is a little more difficult, because the whole body wants to move along with it, but staying seated will help you feel the muscles you have to work in order to isolate this area and draw a circle that little by little gets bigger and bigger. Now, stand up to make circles with the hips, maintaining a liberating contact with the ground, with knees bent and feet parallel. Change to the other direction and if you want, you can change the speed as well: do a few slow circles, and then some faster ones.

Just think that when we belly dance, we use all of these movements, as well as other circles, which require even more control and awareness of the body, because they are drawn on the body's vertical plane. For example, instead of going around from side to side, the hips can draw a circle starting at the top, and then rolling to the front. In this way, the circle becomes a wheel that moves forward. The beauty of these movements lies in their fluidity and variety. You could do a whole dance based just on the circle, thanks to the specific intertwining of the aspects that inspire this symbol.

The circle was one of the first female symbols, contrasting with the line or cross that stands for the masculine spirit.

Very eloquent in and of itself, the circle helps us identify with the various forces it represents. The circle was one of the first female symbols, contrasting with the line or cross that stands for the masculine spirit. Cyclical reality is expressed through belly dancing, and also in the rhythm of the expansion and contraction of the belly, as with the typical undulations (sometimes called "the camel"). Expansion is the cyclical moment of growth and fullness in the belly-circle, which happens during the inhalation of air. Contraction happens when we empty out our lungs, and is the cyclical state of rest, the return to the center, to the navel. A dance well done creates the right relationship between expansion/inhalation, and relaxation/exhalation. For this reason, it is important to slowly feel this movement and give yourself time to breathe.

In this pattern of opposites, inhalation/exhalation, expansion/contraction, lies the inherent sensuality of belly dancing, the typical abandon we see in its moves, where there is a hidden balance between the strength required to execute the movements, and the relaxation of the body: opposites.

The circle is a symbol that draws from completeness: positive and negative aspects. It embraces that which is high, and that which is low, whatever is near, and whatever is far away. The circle is a perfect symbol that embraces the whole; it could be seen as the balanced fusion of male and female, as with the symbol of the yin and yang, or the double circle or sign of infinity, the figure 8- this too is used heavily in belly dancing- which represents, among many things, the sexual union and sense of perfection in two that become one.[1]

As an expression of the feminine principle, the circle can be found in the fullness of the pregnant belly and in the circular movement. One of the meanings of the Hebrew word cholelthi is to spin in a circle, like in a dance, or even in labor, and the word chola- dancing in a circle- can also mean to give birth,[2] a significant connection in the relationship between belly dancing and the birth rite.

> The circle is a perfect symbol that embraces the whole; it could be seen as the balanced fusion of male and female, as with the symbol of the yin and yang, or the double circle or sign of infinity, the figure 8.

In my dance groups, I prefer to use the circle formation, because it's associated with the idea of the "magic circle" or protective circle that recalls the trench surrounding tribal territories, a sort of protection belt that marked the sacred area belonging to the group.[3] The circle is also a very egalitarian formation, because all of the members can be seen and are the same distance from the center. The centric energy gets everyone involved and aims at creating a union and teamwork among the members.

Another very well-known circular dance is that of the mawlaiyya dervishes (mevlevi), which we know as whirling dervishes, and it's inspired by a cosmic symbolism where the dancers imitate the planets' orbits around the sun, the vortex of everything that moves, and also the search for God.

The Circle

This unifying quality is very important in an art that forming "soloists" can sometimes isolate people as they are dancing. It remains a constructive formation, because it discourages jealousies and divisions that can sometimes come between members of the group.

Not by chance, the circle is a very ancient formation: circles of rocks, and circular dances seemed to be a living depiction of all the cycles of the cosmos and life. The practice of dancing in a circle may date back to Paleolithic era, and continued on through the Neolithic. *Girotondi* of naked women appear on the *cucutene* ceramics from the 5th millennium B.C, depicted in a ritual circle with arms linked. These vases are called "Hora vases," just like the circular dance that is still performed today.[4]

The ritual, circular dance that re-created eternal rhythm and the circle of life is overthrown by the medieval images of a macabre dance and in the witches' sabba with the devil.

The circularity of belly dancing is represented as a regenerating energy by the symbols that melt into one another: circles, spirals, figure 8's, snake motions, and whirlpools that stimulate the process of change in a fluid and continuous dance. Another circular object connected to the magic circle is the belt that belly dancers tie around their hips and over time it has become an indispensable accessory.

WORKS CITED IN CHAPTER 3.6

1. B. Walker, *The Woman's Dictionary of Symbols and Sacred Objects*.
2. B. Walker, *The Woman's Dictionary of Symbols and Sacred Objects*.
3. A. Carotenuto, *Jung e la cultura del XX secolo*.
4. M. Gimbutas, *Il linguaggio della Dea*.

3 . 7

(photo: M. Grazia Sarandrea).

5 The Belt around our Hips

The Belt around Our Hips

The belt is a very characteristic complement of belly dancing; a band around our hips is the first accessory we put on before starting to dance. It not only follows in the spiral movement making it more obvious to the eye, but also makes the belly and hips stand out, framing them, and bringing wanted attention to the center of the body- not only the attention of the audience, but also of the dancer herself, who responds to the belt's echoing invitation to focus on the movements of the belly.

The belt not only follows in the spiral movement making it more obvious to the eye, but also makes the belly and hips stand out, framing them, and bringing wanted attention to the center of the body.

The showy, dazzling symbol of the belt comes down to us as a ritual echo of the ancient world. In it is hidden the archaic idea that life, immortality, and sacredness are found in the center, the belly, the fulcrum of fertility. As a symbol of fertility, the belt is connected to our sexuality and the powerful energy that it imprisons in the fertile belly: undone, it correspond to a promise, and fastened it symbolizes refusal.

Belts have always been linked to fertility and birth. For the Greeks and Romans, it was customary for new brides to wear a belt which the husband would then unfasten in bed, as good luck for many children.[1] The belief in "wonder belts" was also well-known; they were thought to facilitate childbirth and were condemned by the council as tools of magic.[2] The connection between belts and fertility is also preserved in the Christian sects, which have worshiped various relics of the Virgin's belt for centuries, hoping to free themselves from the curse of infertility. Another noteworthy belt is that of Queen Puabi of ancient Ur, in south Iraq, about 2500 years before Christ. It was made of gold, lapis, and carnelian. It not only represented her regal power, but was also called the "belt of birth," because it fell at the belly and was said to help carry on the future of humanity.

The belt is a typical feature on the nude figurines of ancient Europe from the 6th to 4th millennia B.C. It had a protective function that was probably derived from its significance as a circle, in that it contained something, and it was a symbol of strength and fidelity.

The ancient Babylonians and Arabs called the constellations of the zodiac the "houses of the moon," while the zodiacal band was known as the "belt of Ishtar," in reference to the ancient, matriarchal religions' lunar calendar, which gave the Goddess control over time, fertility, and human fate or destiny.

The belt was also a symbol of the source of all graces. For instance, the belt of Venus/Aphrodite was thought to contain every type of charm, and was described as a divine amulet that brought all irresistible powers to the woman, so much that Homer said, "…not even the wisest of the wise men could resist them."[3]

It's also worth noting for the study of belly dancing's symbols, that there are maternal signs that still remain in our romance languages linking the belt with fertility: words like incinta or enceinte use the belt to indicate the state of pregnancy.[4]

The Belt and Menstruation

A s a symbol of fertility, there is a connection between the belt and the menstrual cycle, as in the Egyptian symbol of "the blood of the Goddess" or "the blood of Isis" (tit), which was believed to be sacred. "Oh Isis! May your blood live on!" was the invocation of eternity made to the goddess. In the tombs they left amulets in the form of tit, carved from carnelian, a red gemstone.

Originally, the "blood of the Goddess" was a menstrual bandage symbolic of divinity itself. For this reason, the amulet was a particularly precious symbol of life blood, immortality, purity, and strength, and it was often found on the belts of important people.[5]

Also in Greece, the primordial energy of female blood united with the power of the snake and became the magic red belt. It brought magical strength to the divinity and had power over life, death, and rebirth. [6]

WORKS CITED IN CHAPTER 3.7

1. J. Chevalier, A. Gheerbrandt, *Dizionario dei Simboli*.
2. J. Chevalier, A. Gheerbrandt, *Dizionario dei Simboli*.
3. J. Chevalier, A. Gheerbrandt, *Dizionario dei Simboli*.
4. M. Warner, *Sola fra le donne*.
5. C. Pont-Humbert, *Dizionario dei simboli, dei riti e delle credenze*.
6. J. Voss, *La luna nera*.

3.8

(photo: C. Ferrara).

The Spiral's
Cyclical Manifestation

The Spiral's

The spiral is the secret to belly dancing's incredible fluidity, and in particular, to the beauty of the veil dance.

The spiral is the secret to belly dancing's incredible fluidity, and in particular, to the beauty of the veil dance. It's the extra movement that distinguishes belly dancing from other dances. It's the factor that imperceptibly unites all of the dance's elements. To understand better, the body's version of the spiral is the twisting that we do for example, when we are driving and we turn around to back the car up, twisting the upper body back while the lower body stays straight.

This twisting of the upper body is the same movement we use in belly dancing to do spins or to carry the body in one direction or another, as in the veil dance. It makes the dance fluid, continuous, and full of breath. But the spiral can also be done with the lower body, as when we do "the twist," and bring one hip forward and then the other, to the beat of the music. It creates a rustling of the fringe or band that we wear around our hips.

Spiral movements allow us to rest and keep us in shape, maintaining a young and agile body. They help keep the spinal column flexible and straight with passing time, and keep the right amount of space between the vertebrae, especially in the lumbar zone. The spiral is one of the figures that the human body naturally follows. We can see it in the free motions of children as they play. It's the same nature that gives us so many beautiful examples of spirals in the wild: vines, weeds, snails, sea shells.

With belly dancing, the spiral movement ensures us a smooth passage from one move to another, from one side to the other, from up high to down low, and vice versa.

With belly dancing, the spiral movement ensures us a smooth passage from one move to another, from one side to the other, from up high to down low, and vice versa. The spiral not only unites the different movements in space, but also constantly unites the extremities of the body, intensifying the energy: the arms, the hands, and the upper body with the feet, the legs and the hips of the lower body, and the belly button always acting as the center.

The spiral recalls the formation of a certain force, growth; it's an open and optimistic motion. It immediately recalls the idea of a circular movement beginning at the center, coming from the navel and stretching out into infinity.

This figure takes the necessary power from the land for the right grounding (which we spoke about in reference to the land as a symbol) and it flows in a natural, vertical vortex, from high to low and vice versa, making sure that the end of one movement coincides with the beginning of another.

This beautiful symbol is a hymn to joy and life, because it exemplifies the development and energy of nature itself. Through the vortex, nature expresses emanation, extension, development, cyclical continuity in progress, the rotation of creation, and the permanence of life in mobility and through the fluctuations of change.[1]

As the expression of energy and cyclical time, it's a primordial symbol that had already appeared in the Paleolithic era. The early humans associated it with animals of the serpent form, and depicted energy with shapes showing continuous movement. These elements awaken the power calmed by life, and recognize all the centers of life and fertility.

The spiral recalls the formation of a force; it exemplifies the energy and development of nature, which expresses through its vortexes emanation and the cyclical continuity in progress. As a symbol, it had already appeared in the Paleolithic era, where it was associated with serpent-formed animals. In this picture there are spiral designs that change into plants.

This surprising metaphor of nature's vital force, is displayed in the pictures of spirals that change themselves into plants, as in the art from Malta, and Minoan Crete. Spiral dances that wind and unwind were surely practiced in prehistoric times. There is a dance that the crane does, which according to Plutarch, Theseus introduced to Delus: it was performed around an altar with a horn, and it represented the circles that wind and unwind in the labyrinth.[2] As an image of life, the spiral can also be compared to Egyptian amulets and tomb paintings, where it takes on the hope of reincarnation.[3] For the Greeks and Romans, decorations in the form of a spiral or swastika were used as talismans to ward off evil.[4]

The ascending and descending movement of the spiral must have been compared to the moon's spiral, the increasing and decreasing over the course of a month. In this way, it is also connected to the cosmic symbolism of the moon. As a cosmic symbol of change, the spiral is also an erotic symbol of the vulva and fertility and it verifies all the centers of life and fertility.

The Goddess bears a spiral form in her genital triangle, that continuously goes up and down. She is the "lady of life and death," Mother Earth, mother of life, who protects all that has sprung forth from her. And after death it all returns to the earth's womb to be born again, ensuring the perpetual nature of life in a spiral that moves the cyclical wheel of time from death to life.

The spiral is also a symbol of birth, as we can see in the headdress of the Goddess Meskhent. She was identified with the stones that women squatted on while giving birth, and also helped in judging the dead. Her headdress was a symbolic stalk or stem that finished in two spirals, probably meant to look like the umbilical cord, which has a spiral form and unites mother and child. Similarly, the Sumerian Mami, priestess of the Goddess of childbirth, helped women as they began to feel contractions and stayed with them until the moment of birth to predict the future of the newborn.[5]

As a motive of vital force and growth, the spiral is connected to another symbol of life, the breast. We'll see it in the ceramic mammary vases of the Neolithic period, where the nourishing flow of milk was represented with wavy lines.

This spiral, from the headdress of the Egyptian Goddess, Meskhent, was a symbol of birth.

Curiously enough, the spiral is a figure that spontaneously appears during certain phases of meditation, or to people who are asleep in mid-air. Since antiquity, spiral images have been used to indicate the dissolving of the conscious into the darkness of non-being, which express an analogy of the rites of passage with the mystery of birth.[6]

WORKS CITED IN CHAPTER 3.8

1. J. Chevalier, A. Gheerbrandt, *Dizionario dei Simboli.*
2. M. Gimbutas, *Il linguaggio della Dea.*
3. M. Lurker, *Dizionario dei simboli e delle divinità egizie.*
4. J. Chevalier, A. Gheerbrandt, *Dizionario dei simboli.*
5. P. Monaghan, *Le donne nei miti e nelle leggende.*
6. J. Campbell, *Mitologia primitiva.*

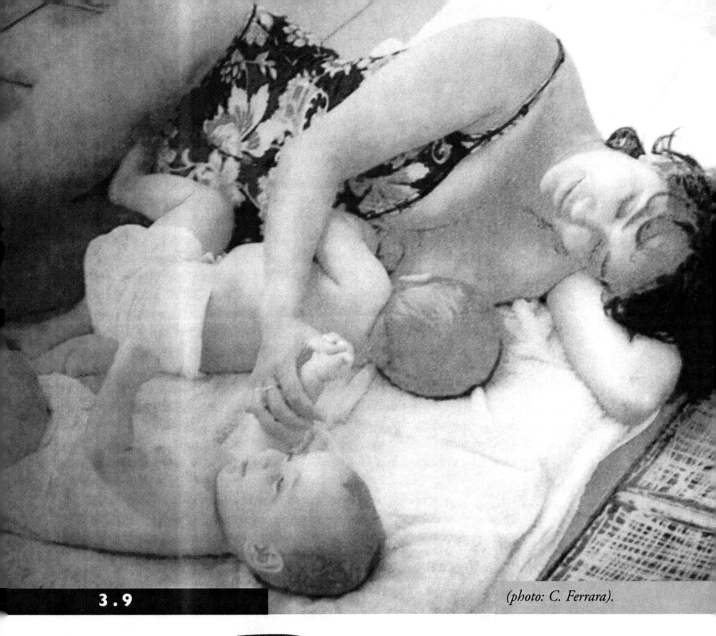

3.9

(photo: C. Ferrara).

7 The Breast
Sustainer of Life

Breast

Ishtar, Goddess of fertility and abundance, Sumerian representation, c. 2000 B.C.

The image of the full, well-rounded breast is certainly exalted by the costumes used in belly dancing. That "prominent accomplice" as Malek Chabel calls it, is a symbol tied to eroticism and sexual attraction. In the dance, there are shoulder undulations, gentle shakes, and back arches that all lift the chest and open up a means of expression that doesn't exclude the sensual aspect of life. As women and dancers, we are aware of this.

Apart from the aspect that identifies the breast with sexual desire more than anything else, there are also other feminine aspects of the breast's beauty that have less resonance in history. For example, its characteristic of giving sustenance for life, or its attribute of being a sacred shelter- these are aspects that originally enriched belly dancing's symbolism and that don't separate the body's sensual experience from its spirituality, even during times when there doesn't appear to be any connection, such as with dancing and breastfeeding.

The most ancient image of mother nursing child brings us back to the Goddess worship, when the sacred attribute of the breast that "gives to the outside," showed her as the mother that gives nourishment, awareness and immortality to the world. In Egypt, the pharaoh sat at Isis's breast and it was thought that this could bring him to a new life in the divine world. The Goddess's belly was considered to be the royal throne, and from her breast flowed the nectar that brought divine rule to the kingdom; so, starting with the first dynasty, the pharaohs always had themselves depicted at the breast of Isis, as they sucked out their divine right to rule the empire.[1]

Thanks to the milk of the Capitoline wolf, the "mother of the Romans," and symbol of the city of Rome, the twin brothers Romulus and Remus were able to survive and found the city. Capitoline Museums (5th century B.C.).

The Breast- Sustainer of Life

The Egyptian hieroglyph mena is the design of a breast, and means breast as well as moon. It reflects the belief that the Milky Way flowed from the breast of the Moon Goddess, and that its stars and water of the Universe gave us life. Something supported by all languages is that "Ma-Ma" means "maternal breast. Another curious little piece of information is that the way we move our heads when we say "yes" or "no" (which is common to almost all languages- only the words change) is natural action learned from breastfeeding. This movement is tied to human breastfeeding and is free of cultural of geographical distinction: nodding "yes," a gesture of well-being and satisfaction, is what babies do when they are being nursed, and shaking the head "no" and pulling away from the breast shows that they are either done or don't want it at all.

The Canaanite Astarte, Goddess of fertility and life. The body parts like the breasts, navel, and pubic area weren't seen as just physical organs, but sacred centers, linked with sexuality. The entire naked body, which was the usual way of representing the divinities, was a form of divine epiphany. Gold plate from a prayer site found in Tell-el-Ajjul, c. 16th century B.C.

The sacred image of the Goddess's breast was so important that the Old Testament god, Yahweh, was given the title "El Shaddai," which means "the breast that nurses," or "mother that nurses." The breast, seen as a symbol of nourishment is reinforced by hundreds of terra cotta models of the feminine figure with the arms drawing attention to either the breasts or the belly. These works of art verify the importance of both body parts in the ancient religions' cults.

The divinity's body and body parts weren't considered to be just physical organs, but sacred centers, linked with sexuality. For this reason, the depictions of the Goddess's body, the exposure of the breasts and belly, or of the entire naked body, was a form of divine epiphany.[2] And it had the same significance in ancient Crete: uncovering the breasts was thought to be a sacred act, and it played a part in the cults where the priestesses showed their full breasts which symbolized the vital flow that provides nourishment. This idea is also supported by the ancient Arabic tradition which asked the women praying with reverent devotion to uncover their right breasts before saying these words: "With my right breast and my sad heart, I beg you to help me."

But the breast is also a refuge, and like all maternal symbols, a promise of fertility and reproduction. The return to the breast of the land marks, like every death, the prelude to a new birth.

This is tied to another symbol that concerns us: Milk, the most first nourishment, the primordial, vital sustenance, which had a fruitful mythology, as with the Roman Goddess, Latona (from the Greek Leto or Leda). In Arabia there was Al-Lat, the Goddess of milk, and childbearing. In the Latopolis temple in Egypt, milk was used as a baptismal liquid. [3]

The Breast

In the language of the Canaanites (one of the many pre-Israelite populations in Palestine) lat meant "Goddess," and the island of Malta was consecrated to this Goddess in her oldest form of Ma Lata.

Milk is associated with images of intimacy, offering, the gift of shelter, and the fortune of rebirth in the way the Egyptians intended it to be when they brought jars of milk into their tombs. [4]

Water is a symbol equivalent to milk. In some of the European cults that used therapeutic practices, springs, fountains, and wells were famous for filling mothers with milk and were the destinations of very long pilgrimages.

Now let's take a look at a lesser-known aspect of belly dancing: its connection with breastfeeding.

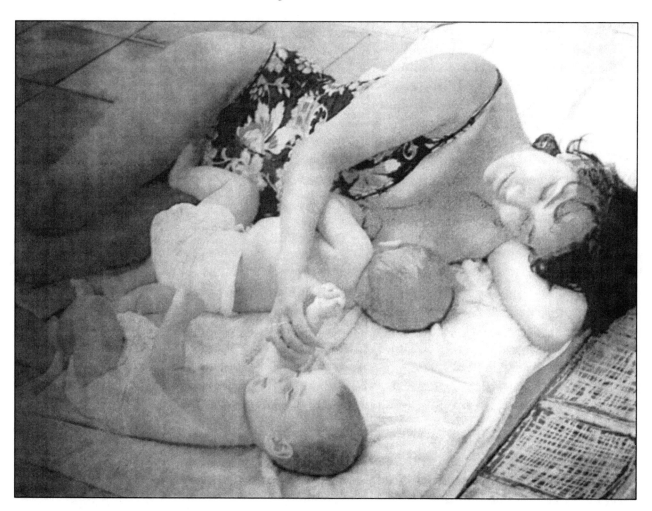

*«I feel my limbs become splendid upon contact with this universe of life.
And my pride is born from the raging of generations
that move rhythmically in my blood at this very moment.».*

Tagore, Gitanjali, *LXIX*

The Breast- Sustainer of Life

Belly Dancing and Breastfeeding

I would like to talk about the practical relationship between belly dancing and breastfeeding. I teach women about nursing in my post-partum classes, and I also breastfed my children for a long time, so I know that belly dancing can greatly enrich the experience that a mother has with nursing. First of all, many of the shoulder movements in belly dancing also involve the chest and naturally help with breastfeeding in that they relax the entire area and draw positive attention to the breast's function as a sustainer of life. In a completely spontaneous way, these movements aid in the production of milk. In fact, I jokingly refer to some of the moves as "milk 1" or "milk 2" in my childbirth preparation courses, knowing that they will help the new mothers with this delicate task that is often not given enough attention, considering that it's a natural function of life.

Breastfeeding is hard work and an art at the same time. It requires time, patience, instinct, and adequate preparation, both mental and physical. But nursing is also very enjoyable: in the sensuality of the body that gives nourishment, in the tight embrace it creates between mother and child, and in the time it gives you to look at your child at length and dream about him or her growing up.

Breastfeeding can even enrich our sex lives, because it develops a greater sensitivity and re-awakens the breasts.

Many of the shoulder movements in belly dancing also involve the chest and naturally help with breastfeeding. (photo: M.G. Sarandrea)

The Breast

Breastfeeding can even enrich our sex lives, because it develops a greater sensitivity and re-awakens the breast. I think this is an important thing to consider, especially for those who think that breastfeeding "damages" the breast, when in reality, it could tune-up its receptiveness.

Although I nursed my children (my daughter and then my twins) for about a year, I don't want to state that all women should breastfeed for a long time. I just think that every woman should be aware of the advantages of breastfeeding in order to decide how much time she might want and might be able to dedicate to it. Of course, we have to consider our obligations at work and the organization of the household, in such a way that whoever wants to nurse, will be able to reserve a good part of her energy for it, because as I said before, it's hard work.

It was very important for me to nurse my children, and it's one of the things that I share with a certain amount of pride, hoping to reassure other women who would like to do the same.

As far as nursing twins goes, there is very little information available, because usually we don't even imagine that one mother could be able to nurse both of them. "How are you going to do that? You'll certainly have your work cut out for you," my friends and acquaintances said to me, and they immediately took it for granted that I wasn't going to breastfeed the twins, and that I would put them on the bottle right away. But as with all arts, there are secrets and tricks. I'll tell you about them in hopes of encouraging those who feel alone or afraid as they await the baby's birth, or those who discover that they are expecting twins, or anyone who is curious about the subject of maternity. I found out that I was pregnant with twins when I had my sonogram and amniotic exam during my fourth month; I was shaken up and a little angry, because I wasn't expecting it.

I was in particular need of inspiration: without knowing that I would later receive double the hugs and kisses, I was just afraid of having double the difficulty delivering two babies and then managing them both at the same time. I never thought I would be able to bring a daughter and two sons into this world; I was afraid I'd have to give up my job forever, and that my body would simply become deformed. Both my husband Calogero, and my obstetrician Ornella, helped me face the undertaking with serenity. And belly dancing also helped me during this vulnerable period, in discovering the incredible abilities of my body. My belly was keeping two little beings alive inside of it, and my breasts prepared themselves to receive them. I let my dancing change according to my body's needs, month after month, without forcing anything, or daring to take new choreographic challenges. I continued to teach and even to performed, dancing on TV during my eighth month of pregnancy. I danced until the night that my babies were born. Usually I followed the music of the flute or violin with a slow tempo, but at the end I danced to percussive music hoping to induce labor, because unlike the pregnancies that don't go full term- six or seven months- which seems to be expected with twins, my boys gave no sign of wanting to come out of their "tranquil," cozy abode.

I let my dancing change according to my body's needs, month after month, without forcing anything, or daring to take new choreographic challenges.

The rhythmic dance, along with the foot massages that my mother gave me, and maybe even the fear of a medicated delivery, helped me accept this first separation, and finally the contractions came.

As with all deliveries, a good dose of courage was in order. I let myself go with my instinct, following the rhythm of my body, and anchoring myself in my breathing, and after a short delivery, the moment came. I held onto my husband at my right side and my gynecologist, Domenica, at the other, in the same standing position that I had used years before when my daughter was born. The position can be different for every woman, and when she is allowed to choose, she finds her own position that is ideal for her as she gives birth.

I brought Gabriel, the first twin, immediately to my breast, and after a little while, the 45 minute break was over and the contractions for the second twin came. It was as if one brother was calling the other into the world; Gabriel called Leandro, and it was a smooth delivery. I won't say it was a walk in the park…it's hard when you've just given birth to one child, with all the necessary effort, knowing that you're not done and that you still have another one on the way… I would have liked a whole day of rest. But nature gives us incredible resources, and I gave birth without complications. It was only after the second delivery that I looked at both of them in peace, losing myself in their two little faces, and after some difficulty and lots of tears, I began to learn how to double my ability to take care of them.

> I found irreplaceable support in the dance, which helped me recognize my own body after giving birth, and also relieved some of my tiredness.

At home, when I began to dance again in the second month of their infancy, I found irreplaceable support in the dance, which helped me recognize my own body after giving birth, and also relieved some of my tiredness. But most importantly, belly dancing helped me nurse my sons simultaneously, without losing myself in complete desperation, damaging my relationship with my family, or giving up on breastfeeding all together, as often happens. In reality, mother nature shows her stuff when it comes to breastfeeding twins; she offers what is needed with calmness and devotion.

Of course, it wasn't easy; it was actually very tiring. For my husband too, who had to wake up in the middle of the night to help me set the babies up with pillows as I sat myself down to nurse them at the same time. It was helpful to remember that we wouldn't have to do that forever.

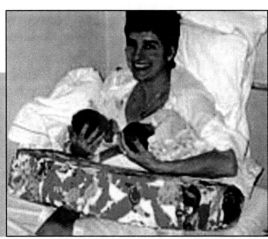

When I nursed the newborn twins, I put their little feet pointing away, and their heads next to each other. You can also put a pillow on your lap, so you don't have to hold them just with your arms. Little by little you find the right position with your back straight and comfortably supported.

The Breast

There are also some little things that you pick up on, the tricks that I mentioned earlier, for example, eating well and often, and not feeling guilty if you don't lose the weight right away. It's important to rest when the babies are sleeping, and take as much help as you can get, without feeling bad. Nurse them both at the same time, even if you have to wake one up, and finally, choose a good position when you're breastfeeding, and take into account the correct positioning of the spine. I found it very helpful to use a bulky, horseshoe-shaped pillow that I wrapped around my waist, so I could put the babies on it at the same time- their little heads on each breast, and their little feet underneath my arms. This method of breastfeeding, the rugby ball position, allowed me to keep my back straight and even free my hands if I wanted to adjust the babies, or sip on a drink.

During pregnancy and early childcare, it's normal to feel like you need extra help, both physical and emotional. I think belly dancing along with the sensual, soft, slow music, and having the positive experience of other women who have already gone through these phases, can be very helpful.

The image of the Goddess inspired me, with her symbols tying the natural world to the miracle of birth. It brings to mind a beautiful statue that I saw at the archeological museum in Syracuse.

She might be "the Night nursing her twins," from a fruitful breast, made of li-

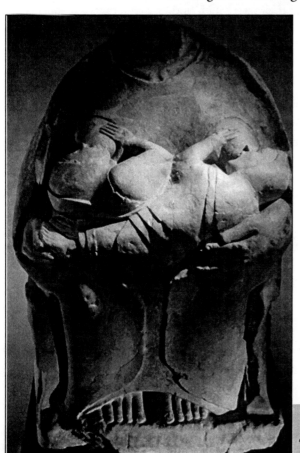

mestone, and very ancient (around 4th century B.C). She was reconstructed in Megera Hyblaiea from countless fragments, and she reminds me of the experience I had with my three children; breastfeeding at night, and the physical and spiritual "reconstruction" that we go through after giving birth.

The beauty of the Goddess is accentuated by the fact that she doesn't have a head, because this advantageous lack puts more emphasis on her generous breast, with which she nurses her twins in a tight embrace. It's millennia old, yet it succeeds in deeply inspiring us, because the language of belly dancing transcends time. In the night-day-night of time, that spins like a wheel, she, "the Night nursing her twins," carries Life forward from the fertile darkness of her belly to the light of birth and her ample breast.

"The Night nursing her twins,"
archeological museum, Syracuse, 4th century B.C.

Fertility and Maternity

The link between fertility and maternity would seem undeniable with all the symbols found in belly dancing, but many authors contest the tendency to look for symbols of fertility everywhere, because they consider that to make it less valuable, or to somehow condense the female experience.

I on the other hand, believe that fertility alludes to the power of the female, which is enclosed in seeds, in creative ideas, and in sexuality. Therefore, it hides a complex symbolism that welcomes different productive aspects of femininity. These touch on creativity in general, the imagination's productivity, the mystery of the body, or the woman's magic ability to offer herself in whatever area of life she chooses to express herself.

I don't believe that the symbols of fertility reduce women to the biological role; on the contrary, I think that it's only the devaluation of the maternal role that makes us consider the symbols of fertility to be too narrow.

When the symbols of fertility refer specifically to maternity, they bring it to new levels, to the point of making this experience common to all people (because we are all born from a woman). This was the pivotal point in the religious intuitions of prehistoric times.

As an art focused on the creative, maternal aspect of life, belly dancing allows us to participate in the essential mystery of life. It's anchored in the matriarchal vision, when the woman was worshiped for her many different traits, primarily that of being maternal. Today belly dancing can help us give positive value to our procreative abilities, and open us to the experience of maternity. I don't think this is a contribution that we should underestimate, because- at least in Italy where there is a worrisome demographic crisis that continues to get worse- it makes us think that a woman's choice to become a mother is more a surrender than a privilege.

In our world, fertility and maternity are presented as topics on the outskirts of culture and the female identity. This lack of importance tends to negatively manifest in the body in the form of different symptoms: disturbed menstrual cycles, anorexia, unofficial infertility, multiple miscarriages, and pregnancy at all costs.[5] These problems express extreme discomfort in society, and suggest that we should restore the balance through maternity.

Belly dancing cultivates femininity in all its forms, starting with the maternal aspect. It is externalized in the body that has real volume, inner depth, and grace. Half symbolically, but also in a practical way, it helps many women face their fears... not so much of childbirth itself, but the transformation of girl to mother, which comes when we give birth.

The dance begins its approach with the body, through its symbols, which in the end, are symbols of Life and Reproduction, based on the maternal figure of the

Fertility is the power of the female, which is enclosed in seeds, in creative ideas, and in sexuality.

The Breast

Goddess of Fertility who gives physical as well as creative nourishment. Through dance, a woman can discover the sacred founts of Life in her body, the spiritual importance of Life.

This new awareness of the body can accentuate the gratification a woman has in being able to accomplish the ultimate act of natural creativity by becoming a mother, or to exalt her creative qualities, her fertile imagination, in the other areas that she chooses to apply herself.

> When a woman dreams about having a child, but is afraid, belly dancing can help her discover the importance of maternity.

When a woman dreams about having a child, but is afraid, belly dancing can help her discover the importance of maternity, not as a pre-established gender role, something that "everyone can do," where there is an implicit devaluation of procreation, but rather, an invitation to experience it as a personal choice, a privilege of femininity, something she can be proud of and take great spiritual satisfaction from. She has to fight for a positive definition of maternity, because when she takes on this role, it may put her at a disadvantage in other spheres of life, particularly in the workplace. Staying in contact with her true femininity, with the "feminine source" of the world, she will find the right balance, because if she knows herself well, she will be able to understand how to manage her time better to distribute her energy with good judgment.

Cultivating a Space for Yourself

> Sometimes women come to dance with me after abandoning their art for many years, either to dedicate themselves completely to work...they gave something up without realizing how much they hurt themselves when they cut out their creative life.

Sometimes women come to dance with me after abandoning their art for many years, either to dedicate themselves completely to work, or because they thought it was better for their children, or because their husbands wanted them to. They gave something up without realizing how much they hurt themselves when they cut out their creative lives. In their eyes I can see a terrible emptiness- I'm not exaggerating- a deep suffering. Even if there is a certain stretch of time when dancing doesn't seem absolutely necessary, eventually that moment of emptiness comes, because art nourishes the soul; it's the heart's food, and at a certain point, we can't go on without it.

When they start dancing again, I see them smiling with satisfaction, even though they might complain about the body having "forgotten everything." I think it's important to surround ourselves with people who support our creativity, and who encourage us in whatever we do. We can't deny our muse without sacrificing our happiness.

Group improvisation at the Omphalos Theater.

In Bari, when I danced for the del Levante fair, a beautiful Egyptian woman of about 40 came to find me after the performance. She was crying, so I asked her why. She told me that she missed her country and she missed dancing, and that I had made her imagine the music again. She asked me if I was Egyptian and if I was married. I explained that I was born in Colombia, but that I had lived in the US and had traveled a lot, and that I finally settled down in Italy when I met my husband and got married.

She seemed very surprised that I was married and yet still continued to dance, and then she told me about how she had been a belly dancer at one time. She had an orchestra of musicians and she traveled the world doing shows; she loved her work, and she made good money.

She told me that she had promised the man she loved that she would give up dancing once they got married. And so she did, and more than twenty years had passed since then. It wasn't a good choice. She made me feel like this kind of sacrifice was as bad as selling your soul to the devil, because it was obvious that she felt like she had lost her true self.

Later we met for lunch at her house, but we ate very quickly, because I couldn't wait to see her dance. I had to be very persistent, but when she finally danced, she was sure of herself; I could tell that she had been a wonderful dancer, and she smiled with all her heart. Before going back to my hotel, she gave me an ornament, a very beautiful and unique pharaoh crown. She told me that I was right in not giving up my art for marriage, as she had done, and she gave me a hug.

It seemed like a story from another time, another place, but there are situations that can always put our creative life at risk. You should never quit dancing, not even for love. It happened to a very talented dancer I worked with back in New

She told me that she had promised the man she loved that she would give up dancing once they got married. And so she did, and more than twenty years had passed since then. It wasn't a good choice. She made me feel like this kind of sacrifice was as bad as selling your soul to the devil, because it was obvious that she felt like she had lost her true self.

It takes a lot of will to give back to yourself, because usually after having children we tend to overlook the body and its emotional needs.

York- her husband was jealous and wanted to keep her from dancing, so he hid all of her costumes in a suitcase and brought it to their friends' house. She was desperate and had no choice but to call all of their friends or go to their houses looking for the clothes. Finally the "costume confiscator" didn't have the heart to deny it anymore when he saw her in tears....

Fortunately, many women have partners who support them and encourage them to develop their art. Actually, there are many men who appreciate the positive effects the dance has on their partners, which then transfer to their relationship. However, it often seems that it's time that acts as tyrant over us. Those who have a family or a job, never have enough time on their hands, especially when it comes to doing something for themselves.

Sometimes the mothers that come to my classes talk about the difficulties we have cultivating an art and taking care of the family at the same time. I'm familiar with the effort and organizational skills it takes to find a couple hours a week to come to lesson, so it gives me great pleasure to offer them a prosperous space in which to take care of themselves and grow.

It takes a lot of will to give back to yourself, because usually after having children we tend to overlook the body and its emotional needs; but we mothers need to recharge in order to have something to offer others. Without feeling like we're taking time away from the family, we deserve a little time dedicated to taking care of ourselves.

Most importantly, for the women who are used to always putting the needs of others before their own, this is an important space they can keep to themselves.

There's time for everything, even if it's not all at once; in fact, every time that I've tried to be super mom I ended up exhausted and misunderstood.

I don't think there's a good recipe for time management, but each one of us has to find the right balance between the time dedicated to the family and/or work, and the time dedicated to ourselves. This balance is different for every woman and every mother. How can a mother raise her children well if she stays at home all the time feeling unhappy about the fact that she doesn't go to work or dance or do anything for herself? By the same token, what can a mother offer if she works all the time and feels guilty about not being home with her children? There's time for everything, even if it's not all at once; in fact, every time that I've tried to be super mom I ended up exhausted and misunderstood. In my case, I have to try to balance my family, my art, and my career. But I don't think of them as different streets that exclude each other and create problems. For the most part, maternity makes a woman better, more complete, and more mature, and these qualities that we acquire can also be applied to work and dance.

WORKS CITED IN CHAPTER 3.9

1. S. Husain, *La Dea.*
2. E. Neumann, *La grande madre.*
3. B. Walker, *The Woman's Dictionary of Symbols and Sacred Objects.*
4. J. Chevalier, A. Gheerbrandt, *Dizionario dei Simboli.*
5. S. Vegenti Finzi, *Volere un figlio.*

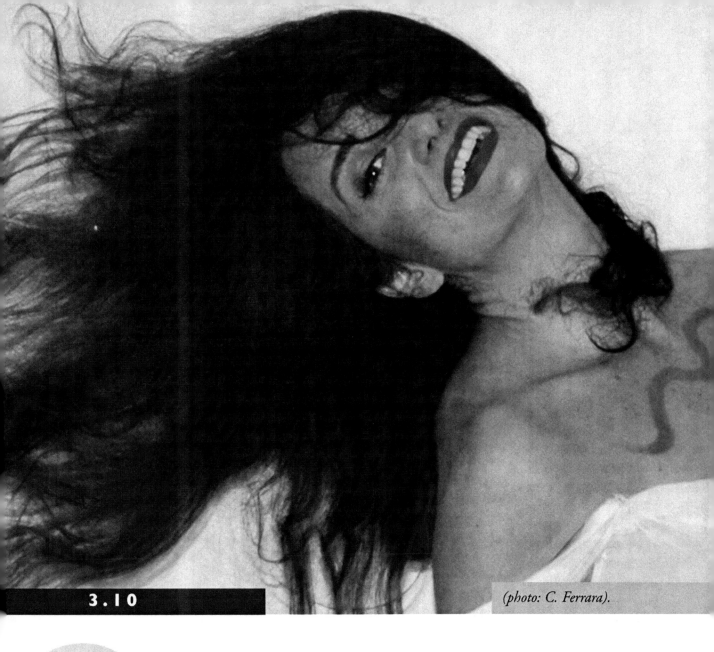

3.10

(photo: C. Ferrara).

8 The Hair

The Hair

«…es hora de que me muestres
lo que sabes hacer.
Abrete, suèltate
El pelo Enmaranato,
sube y quema
las alturas del cielo».

«…it's time you show me
what you know how to do.
open yourself, let
your hair down,
jump up and burn
the heights of the sky».

P. Neruda, Odas elementales.

One of the things I love to do before beginning a lesson is to ask the women to let their hair down. It's an action that seems very simple but sometimes they fight it. We all tend to worry too much about how we look, being put together, having a fresh, polished appearance and so on. But letting our hair down means letting ourselves go. It opens us up to our own femininity and natural instinct. I'd like to think that it also opens us up to our inner wild child. It feels good to express ourselves, even though this can sometimes mean letting other people see us when our appearance is less than perfect. Using your hair while you dance is a liberating action that makes you completely uninhibited. For this reason, we shouldn't underestimate the importance of letting our hair flow freely while we dance, and we should include it in our moves. Something changes in the dance's character as the experience that the dancer has with her body's potential changes. The hair is like our original veil; we can hide behind it or reveal something about ourselves. Sometimes the hair also helps creative ideas come to us when we let ourselves go with our instinct and leave our hair down and wild. Letting our hair down is an action that frees us from many constraints. This is even true for women with short hair, who often think that they won't be able to use their hair while they dance. But it really has to do with this: being able to create a safe environment where we can discover the sensuality of the body and overcome many taboos.

To make this task easier, I begin by working on slow breathing for a long time while we focus our concentration on the muscles of the neck and face, where a lot of tension usually accumulates. Through relaxation, we come closer to feeling the sensuality hidden in this region of the body, which we are not used to expressing very often. Sometimes I dim the lights to create a more intimate atmosphere, which helps when I ask the women to let themselves go with the movement of the head and the hair. Then I propose different figures for them to make with their hands, just as with the different rotations of the head, and we keep going until the whole body is involved. I know that this exercise has worked when the dancers feel comfortable and start having fun, continuing to dance in this way, and improvising on their own. They find a rhythm more adapted to their own needs, that can either be powerful and wild, or very slow and sensual. Interpreting belly dancin-

Using your hair while you dance is a liberating action that makes you completely uninhibited. For this reason, we shouldn't underestimate the importance of letting our hair flow freely while we dance, and we should include it in our moves. Something changes in the dance's character as the experience that the dancer has with her body's potential changes.

g's music and gestures in this specific way, every woman can offer her own personal revelation. As a spectator of my students' dancing, I find that these movements are very graceful. They are able to express themselves freely and femininely, without faking it, and this is one of the reasons that makes me love my job.

The greatest wish that I could have for a dancer is that she might lose herself in the dance, being able to feel the inspiration that lets you abandon yourself to something bigger than you. That's when you feel the chill that makes your hair stand on end and gives you goose-bumps, and sometimes it comes to you like an unexpected gift. The early humans were no strangers to this divine experience that they found through the primitive forms of belly dancing. In fact, in the ancient religions, the Goddess was identified with the landscape and sacred nature; the grass and the plants were her hair, and they were respected and even played a part in different rituals dedicated to her.

Smohalla, the wise-man of the Umatilla tribe, gave a celebrated account when the hunting territory was taken away from his people and they were forced to change their means of survival: "You ask me to cut the grass and grain and to sell them in order to profit like the white man does. But how could I dare cut my mother's hair?"

In the woman's hair there are hidden powers of protection, resurrection, and the reincarnation of the divinity. In hieroglyphic writings, "mourning" was represented by three strands of hair.[1]

> *The Egyptian hieroglyph for "mourning" was a picture of three strands of hair. The legend says that the Goddess Isis, in mourning for Osyris-Horus, cut a strand of hair and then brought him back to life by brushing her hair over him.*

The legend says that the Goddess Isis, in mourning for Osyris-Horus, cut a strand of hair and then brought him back to life by "brushing her hair over him." When participating in the ritual dance honoring the Goddess, the women untied their hair. Similarly, a woman giving birth also kept her hair down to symbolize that everything had to be loose and open to facilitate the delicate passage.

The comb, an object most commonly associated with the hair, was an important symbol of the feminine, connected to the control of time. In fact, the Greek word for comb, *kteis*, also means vulva, which in the matriarchal vision was a symbol of life and reproductive energy.

However, the hair is also a symbol of masculine vitality. The Babylonian myth of Gilgamesh tells us that he had long hair, but lost it when he got sick. He then had to face the challenge of a long journey, so that he would be able to grow his hair out again and return to his homeland reinvigorated. The hair is also a symbol of royalty and power, as we can see in the word "Caesar" and its derivatives, "Kaiser," "Czar" which literally mean "with long hair."

The greatest wish that I could have for a dancer is that she might lose herself in the dance, being able to feel the inspiration that lets you abandon yourself to something bigger than you. That's when you feel the chill that makes your hair stand on end and gives you goose-bumps, and sometimes it comes to you like an unexpected gift.

The hair is also a symbol of royalty and power, as we can see in the name "Caesar", which literally means "with long hair".

The Hair

Let's not forget Delilah, "the one who makes men weak." She cut Samson's hair to take away his strength. Coincidentally, Samson was named after Shans-On, the Arabic God of the sun, whose myth tells how he sacrificed his hair to the Moon Goddess.

At one time, braids of hair were offered to the female deity. We can still see traces of this practice in the form of braided breads, which once substituted the Germanic women's tradition of cutting their hair in offering to the Goddess Berchta or Perchta. The braid is also a symbol of the amorous bond; it is a sweet twisting that binds the loved one, as we see in the *Song of Songs*:

«…the purple hair on your head has captured a king in its braids! How enchanting you are, how charming you are, my delicious love!».

The hairstyle is one of a woman's sensual symbols, so there is a particular importance in whether it is visible or hidden, tied back or let down. It has been a symbol of a woman's availability, either of her invitation or reservation.

The hairstyle is one of a woman's sensual symbols, so there is a particular importance in whether it is visible or hidden, tied back or let down. It has been a symbol of a woman's availability, either of her invitation or reservation.

In certain periods, hair that was worn down in public was characteristic of "loose women," and having their heads shaved was one of the public punishments they had to suffer. Covering the head was a common custom even for our Western culture up until a few decades ago. The idea of sexual provocation being related to a loose and flowing hairstyle is the origin of a woman's obligation to cover her head, especially when entering sacred places.[2]

The hair can be a symbol of the availability or reservation of a woman, or of a spiritual offer, as in this sculpture of the penitent Mary Magdalene, where she is covered only by her hair.

The hair has also been associated with negative powers. During the Inquisition, it was believed that witches created storms when they lost or combed their hair. It is also known that Joan of Ark's short hair that waved in the wind was a deciding factor in her death sentence. After all, this couldn't have been the hair of a woman who claimed to be working for God.[3]

Removing the hair completely was a very important initiation rite, because a shaved head looks like both a skull and the head of a newborn; it therefore emphasizes the implications of death and rebirth, the very rites of passage. The tonsure haircut probably originated from a Babylonian custom of shaving part of their slaves heads,[4] or maybe as Neumann claims, it was a typical practice for the followers of the Great Mother, the bald priests of the Goddess Isis.[5]

Since hair is located at an extremity of the body, and since it is separate from the body, in that we can cut it and grow it out again and again, it represents a vital force and is in constant relationship with the essence of human life. For the Islamic people, hair represents a mediator between the visible and invisible.

Hair was used in spells and it was believed that it retained its close connection to the person even

Three woman with long hair. Photograph: Belle Johnson, c. 1900, Ohio.

after it had been cut. Hair that was cut or ripped out by a comb wasn't thrown away, because it could have been used in magic ceremonies that could have caused harm to the owner.[6]

As a constantly renewing part of the body, hair is linked to another symbol of eternal movement, the snake. The horrifying heads of the Gorgons exemplify this link perfectly. They were represented as three sisters: Steno, Euriale, and Medusa.

These monster-women, even though they might have had beautiful faces and beautiful figures, were horrible to look at. They had scales covering their bodies, their hair was made of slithering snakes constantly moving, and their eyes could turn a person to stone in just one glance.

However, many scholars see a connection between the Gorgons (before this frightful image from Greek mythology was given to them) and the priestesses of the triple Moon Goddess. These women wore masks and guarded the secrecy of feminine mysteries.[7] The original Gorgons, as Gimbutas claims, were powerful

The hair has also been associated with negative powers. During the inquisition, it was believed that witches created storms when they lost or combed their hair.

The Hair

Goddesses of life and death, and were not the later Indo-European monsters that the heroes like Perseus had to kill.[8]

These Goddesses had the ability to represent complementary opposites, such as creation and destruction, birth and death, and passivity and enthusiasm. Reality is symbolized in the unconscious mind and in mythology by circular figures that represent fullness or completeness, for example, the uroburo, the snake that bites its tail. Just like hair, these symbols of reality constantly renew themselves delivering the message that an end is always followed by a beginning.

The tradition of belly dancers having long flowing hair, affirms the symbolic role attributed to this part of the body: transporters of Life and Energy, symbol of great energy, physical strength, and sensuality.

WORKS CITED IN CHAPTER 3.10

1. M. Lurker, *Dizionario dei simboli e delle divinità egizie.*
2. C. Pont-Humbert, *Dizionario dei simboli, dei riti e delle credenze.*
3. G. Bechtel, *Le quattro donne di Dio.*
4. A. Stevens, *Il filo di Arianna.*
5. E. Neumann, *La grande madre.*
6. J. Chevalier, A. Gheerbrandt, *Dizionario dei Simboli.*
7. P. Monaghan, *Le donne nei miti e nelle leggende.*
8. M. Gimbutas, *Il linguaggio della Dea.*

Medusa. Marble head by Bernini, 1630. Capitoline Museums, Rome.

3.11

(photo: C. Ferrara).

9 "S" for Secret and "S" for Snake

"S" for Snake

At the beginning of my adventure with this book I had a visitor: one morning I was getting ready to bring the twins outside in their carriage, when I opened the door and saw a snake slithering vivaciously. It was so close that it seemed to be knocking on the door! I was so surprised and afraid that I screamed and slammed the door shut. After I recovered from the shock, I thought that maybe this guest could have been a sign of good luck for my research. After all, it's impossible to watch a talented belly dancer with her sinuous, fluid grace and not think of a slithering snake. We might even say she's doing a "snake dance." In fact it's customary for some dancers to use a snake or two in their dances. They either carry them gracefully on their heads, or let them loose around their bodies at the waist or shoulders.

As for me, I don't think I'll ever have the courage or desire to dance *with* a snake. Personally, I prefer to dance *like* a snake, because the characteristics of a snake's movement are fluidity, harmony, and mystery, but more importantly because the snake is a symbol that inspires me and peaks my curiosity.
A question that I think we should ask is: Why do we dance like snakes and not like cats or leopards or horses? I think it could be used as evidence to remind us of the ancient rites of transformation. The symbol of the snake sends us to the most remote periods of history and, like our dance, it brings us back to our origins. These creatures have left an undeniable mark on the history of mankind and have influenced our universal vision and religions.

When I dance, the snake comes to life in my arms, which become fluid and winding.

When I dance, the snake comes to life in my arms, which become fluid and winding. It's in the hands when I let the little movement of my fingers extend and contract to slowly stroke through the space around my body, or when I place one hand on top of the other to make a cobra's head in front of me. Sometimes it's in the penetrating stare I focus on a single point, where I direct all of my movement, or it's in the head when I play with the music and shift it from side to side. It's in the veils that wrap around me and then drop one by one like shedding skin. It's in the water-like fluidity that I look for in my body, or in the ground that supports and accompanies my movements. But surely the part of my body that best represents power of the snake is the spine. With years of practice, the backbone becomes fluid and loose, like that of the snake using its spine to hug the earth and water in a never-ending " s" movement.
Dancing like a snake, I explore space with my senses, with my touch, with my eyes, with my whole body. I remain close to the land, with my knees together, staying very focused. The movement through which I bring the snake to life is slow and it transforms; it goes from one figure to another, without drawing attention to the "seams," or transitions. It's a continuous flow of the whole body that celebrates slowness and the occasional surprise of an outburst.

The symbol of the snake gives us the possibility to express our souls, which manifest mostly in the non-verbal language of the body. It helps us make a home in our bodies, to listen to the body and its needs. The snake is connected to instinct and creativity; it's a very helpful symbol in creating a dance, playing and moving with style, finding the ability to let ourselves go to our natural rhythms.

Its image as a primordial animal invites us to abandon ourselves to intuition, and to not succumb to the dictation of reason. It's an inner discovery that regards the language of the heart and all of our emotions, because "…intuition starts at the heart and, lifting up the veil to that which appears, allows those who listen to get a glimpse at the meaning of life."[1]
In the seminars that I lead on this symbol, I invite the women to observe the snake's movements (if possible in real life, but also in documentaries) and to get rid of the stereotypes connected to it, because as I explain, we can't really understand the characteristic expression of belly dancing, nor the hidden meaning behind its movements, if we reject the snake.

The snake can transmit the Neolithic heritage that shaped our dance if we are willing to look for its positive traits. There is another side to the snake that is unrelated to the repulsion that it inspires in our culture.
To appreciate its symbolism, the customary use of the snake's image is not enough. We have been forced to identify it with negative adjectives like, hypocritical, unfaithful, and deceitful, to the point that when we call someone a snake, we are insulting him or her.

The idea of following an "insulting dance" with my art as a "snake dancer" is far from my intention. This made me realize how important it was to make very clear what the slithering dance meant- if it were offensive to us or others- or, if by giving precedence to the hidden values of this symbol, we could find its nocturnal, overlooked value: the praises rather than the insults.

To get back to this positive, archaic symbolism of the snake, we have to go back to the dawning of mankind, much before the snake came to the Garden of Good and Evil and lost its positive reputation just as Eve did. This is when it became the tool of Satan and the symbol of betrayal that we inherited in our culture. Even later, in the Victorian epoch, Freud dug deep into human nature and "rediscovered" the snake. The primitive symbol remained hidden in his psychoanalytical interpretations, because he favored the associations of the snake with the male principle. Of course, it's natural that we think of the snake as a phallic symbol, but this doesn't mean that we should exclude its worth as a feminine symbol. The relationship between the woman and snake is multifaceted, and it can't be explained universally as a simple erotic symbol.[2] There are some very important aspects that have been forgotten, which have to do with the primitive symbolism of life and regeneration.

The symbol of the snake gives us the possibility to express our souls, which manifest mostly in the non-verbal language of the body.

I think is a wonderful, noteworthy fact that over time, over various transformations and heavy censorship, our snake dance has preserved the feminine archetype of the snake, with its values tied to the origin of life and creativity. Being a very old and complex symbol, I will try to illustrate some of the aspects that concern belly dancing, for example, the snake's form, the characteristics of its movement, the Goddesses that kept it as a companion etc, until I get to the reasons that probably made it the "guide animal" for belly dancing, when it was universally considered to be the "woman's teacher."

The Uroburo

The snake's "form" has more than one characteristic; it can be stiff or flexible, and can be interpreted as a male phallus as well as a female circle, a snake that bites its tail. This second form, the uroburo, is one of the oldest representations of the Great Mother which demonstrated the self- sustaining processes of life, the perfect metamorphosis of life into death and vice versa, in a continuous cycle that serves as the fundamental quality of organic existence on our planet.

The uroburo, as a primordial emblem of creation, is a uterine symbol of our origins that contains the ideas of movement, continuity, and eternal return.

The uroburo, as a primordial emblem of creation, is a uterine symbol of our origins that contains the ideas of movement, continuity, and eternal return. It is the image that best defines the concept of time, the "great circle." This idea was then replaced by the Christian concept of linear time, which is given a be-

The uroburo, a snake biting its tail, is a symbol of the eternal return and the continuous regeneration of life. Miniature Arabic design from the 18th century

ginning - the creation of earth - and an end - the last judgment. In the uro-buro, we can also see the suggestion of male and female principles, which we can understand through this interpretation: the union of opposites, the sexual union, which forms One and pushes the wheel of life and reproduction forward.

The double value of the snake, which is the interpretation that we want to use, makes it a female symbol just as much as male. This is demonstrated by the fact that it represents a womb and phallus at the same time and is a symbol of fertility.

The caduceus- two snakes intertwined- represents the equilibrium reached when opposite forces are integrated. It's one of the oldest and most positive images of the snake and it came down to us as a symbol of Western medicine. It was originally attributed to Isis and Ishtar and later to Hermes.

The Goddesses' Companion

As a fundamental archetype of life and fertility, the snake was the companion of many Mother Goddesses in the Mediterranean and the Near East. Astarte, also known as the Goddess Asthoret in the Old Testament, was depicted with two serpents in one hand, and in the other, a lotus flower and a mirror. It was said that the Mesopotamian Goddess Ishtar was covered with snake-like scales, and Isis, of ancient Egypt, was represented with a sacred cobra on her head: the golden ureo, symbol of divine sovereignty, awareness, life, and youth. Later, Hecate, one of the Greek Goddesses, was the queen of the night and the underworld. She was also part serpent and had magical powers that allowed her to raise the dead and bring nature to life. Artemis, who represented changing female energies, had the same powers as snakes, related to the earth. Persephone, Goddess of the underworld, sat calmly in her cavern creating a tapestry of the whole world while her snakes kept watch. Athena, as much as she was a heavenly Goddess, had a serpent as one of her symbols, as did Cybele, the *Magna Mater* of the Romans.

In ancient Greece, the snake had a very important role in the worship of Asclepius. His name was etymologically connected to the word for trap. The snake wrapped around Asclepius' staff (caduceus) is one of the few positive symbols of the snake that has been passed down to our generation.

The caduceus was also an attribute of the Goddesses Isis, Ishtar, and Igea, and was associated with the worship of Asclepius. His symbol of a snake, along with Panacea, respectively represented the two aspects of health care: prevention, and therapy.[6]

Many Goddesses, such as the Gorgons and Erinne, had snakes for hair. In the city of Eleusi, snakes took part in the rituals to the mother Goddess Demeter, whose followers believed in the idea of rebirth and transformation through a new birth. As a mythical ancestor, the snake Ophione figures into Eurinome's myth of origin, with whom she united to create the universe. Also in Crete, it was thought that the Goddess and her snake were the first couple. The main ritual of the island was the dance of the Snake Goddess, symbol of eternity and immortality.

The snake accompanied all the major nature Goddesses until it was condemned by Yahweh, as we find written in *Genesis*, to slither the earth and eat dust. It was then stomped on and cursed by the Immaculate Conception, when it became an emblem of lust, defeated by the purity and wisdom of the Virgin. At this point, the snake had already lost all of its positive connotations of the archaic Goddess's knowledge and power. Curiously enough, if we look carefully we find that the stomped- upon snake maintains its primitive secret. Despite its negative image in the Christian depictions of Mary, it continues to reveal itself along with other symbols including the moon, the stars, and water, which all communicate the mysteries of life, growth, and birth that belonged to the Goddess and woman in the ancient religions.[8]

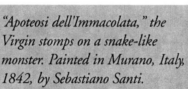

The most famous sculpture of either the Minoan Snake Goddess or one of her priestesses, c. 1800 B.C. Heraklion Museum, Crete.

"Apoteosi dell'Immacolata," the Virgin stomps on a snake-like monster. Painted in Murano, Italy, 1842, by Sebastiano Santi.

The Snake's Mysteries

The characteristic qualities of the snake's movement determined many of its meanings in prehistoric times and made it the symbol of energy and pure, simple strength. The fact that the snake could slither vivaciously over land and through water ensured that their worship was just as tied to the symbolism of Life's primordial water, as to the symbolism of the underworld, which represented the regenerative powers of nature. Living underground, the snake could also participate in the mysteries of Life's transformations, and it became a symbol of awareness since it could penetrate all secrets and understand the future.

At the navel-omphalos of Delphi, there was a serpent that was believed to live in the uterus of the earth and possess all wisdom.

Many Hebrew and Arabic words still used today are derived from the magical abilities of the snake, especially words referring to magic.[9]

The snake hibernates and wakes up again, which can be compared to the re-awakening of nature in general. For this reason, ritual festivals took place on a specific day of the year, probably "the day of the snake."[10] Due to its flexible backbone, it can move in a fluid and winding manner. The snake is connected to the symbolism of the spiral and the eternal flow of Life: the dance that has no end to its existence.

Its symbolism regarding life is evident in the similarity of the Arabic words for snake, alhayyah, and life, al-hayat- and also in the single word of the Caldeans which meant both snake and life.[11]

Being the master of the earth's belly, and a sort of belly himself, the snake was "the reviver," because he was thought to be a benevolent creature. Through him, the influx of life was turned into growth, into the energy of ascending movement. It was the means by which nourishment traveled from the roots to the tops of the trees. Combined with magic plants, the powers of the snake were effective in healing and re-creating life.[12]

The characteristic that most influenced the ancient religions was definitely the periodic shedding of the skin, when it traded in the old one for a nice, shiny new one. This attribute made the snake a symbol of immortality, as we see in the Egyptian hieroglyphic for life's eternal movement.[13] In addition to the other characteristics of its movement, this eternal quality inspired snakes to be used in art starting in the Paleolithic era. Its importance then steadily increased throughout the Neolithic era, and finally reached its height in Europe around 5000-4000 B.C.14

> The characteristic that most influenced the ancient religions was definitely the periodic shedding of the skin, when it traded in the old one for a nice, shiny new one.

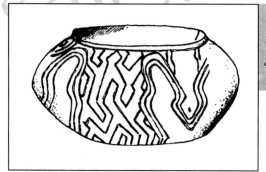

The symbol of the snake inspired prehistoric art in the Paleolithic era and its importance steadily increased throughout the Neolithic era in Europe. Snake head emerging from bands and meandering lines, 6th century B.C.

The Snake and Fertility

Since prehistoric times, or at least since the discovery of agriculture, the snake has been a personification of the moon. Like the moon, it disappears and reappears and is a symbol of eternity, renewal, and also fertility. They were both thought to have power over the fertility of women, and the snake was universally considered to be the "husband of all women," especially during menstruation. They believed that the snake could impregnate them during this time.

For that reason, the women of some tribes didn't go near bushes or water sources when they were menstruating, in fear of being impregnated by a snake. However, the women who wanted to have children often journeyed to a spring where there was said to be a sacred snake.[15] It was also believed that the snake aided in having a smooth delivery and that it discouraged infertility and guaranteed numerous offspring.

The snake's regenerative power was believed to be a creative feminine energy…

The snake's regenerative power was believed to be a creative feminine energy, a lunar energy comparable to that of women- in that they are also in harmony with the moon and have the power to bleed every month without dying.

The snake was also one of the original symbols of female blood, as we can see in the myths of two different cultures. One myth in the Hebrew tradition tells us that when the snake seduced Eve he also caused menstruation. This concept supports the Iranian myth that considered Ahriman, in the form of a snake, to be the one who gave menstruation its origin when he united with the first mother, Jahi.[16]

The essential bond between the snake and menstrual blood, which was considered to be the primary material of human existence in the archaic world, makes it impossible for me to resist the temptation of finding a connection between early belly dancing and the rituals of conception and birth (as we talked about in 2.3 "The Life Blood").

Without exaggerating, we could say that the snake was the totem animal for belly dancing- the sacred animal that helped our dance make its mark in prehistoric times.

The snake was the "animal guide," who our ancestors "became familiar with" through their gestures and the imitation of its "dance." They practiced this dance with the desire to be in complete possession of the sacred qualities of life's processes, reproduction, and birth.

It's very likely that during this era, when the connection between pregnancy and sexual relations had not yet been clearly established, they utilized belly dancing as a reproductive dance. The dance reflected the movement of the snake, and therefore, could have had the same attributes of fertility as those that were given to the snake, which they believed had the power to impregnate women during menstruation.[17] It surely served in invoking the magic necessary for conception, which according to their beliefs, happened because of the transformation of menstrual blood when it coagulated into the human form.

Later, the serpent's positive reputation as the "teacher of women," caused people to believe that it helped carry pregnancy along to the point of delivery. At that point, the snake was probably invoked to get the woman in synch with the rhythms of labor and birth, because it was also thought that the animal "made children be born."[18]

I think the image of the snake as a guide for childbearing is very appropriate, in that birth has similar rhythms. It is the transformation and undulating movement that helps bring a new generation into the world. There is no other moment in life like childbirth when it's more important to follow your animal instinct to be able to do something well.

As a sacred event, childbirth could have also been accompanied by a ritual practiced in the caverns, which were considered to be the "belly of the earth," and therefore, were in synch with the pregnant belly of the woman. Here they welcomed the reproductive energies of the snake and the underground, which could have helped put time in motion and bring about the transformation of the girl who sheds her old skin to become a mother.

The rhythmic undulations of the belly during labor, which help bring the baby into the world, are reminiscent of the snake's "s" movements and are still used in belly dancing as typical undulations and vibrations.

The umbilical cord that connects mother and child also resembles a snake, and the "private sea" where the baby grows can be compared to the primordial water from which the snake emerges. In the same way, the baby emerges from the primordial water of the maternal belly, accompanied by the umbilical snake.

All of these ideas formed the woman's internal music at the dawning of time, and pushed her to start dancing like a snake, as belly dancers do, to invoke life, to feel their bodies, to stay together, and to give birth.

I think it's important to cultivate this wild and primitive aspect that lives in the snake, in an art that has such a far-away echo going back to the origins of hu-

> There is no other moment in life like childbirth when it's more important to follow your animal instinct to be able to do something well.

"S" for Snake

manity and consciousness. This will show us, once again, that we know what to do in both the dance and childbirth- on the condition that we don't shut out our instinctive nature.

WORKS CITED IN CHAPTER 3.11

1. A. Carotenuto, *Il tempo delle emozioni.*
2. M. Eliade, *Trattato di storia delle religioni.*
3. C. Pont-Humbert, *Dizionario dei simboli, dei riti e delle credenze.*
4. A. Stevens, *il Filo di Arianna.*
5. M. Battisti, *Dizionari dell'arte, dei simboli e allegorie.*
6. F. Capra, *Il punto di svolta.*
7. P. Monaghan, *Le donne nei miti e nelle leggende.*
8. M. Warner, *Sola fra le donne.*
9. M. Eliade, *Trattato di storia delle religioni.*
10. M. Gimbutas, *Il linguaggio della Dea.*
11. J. Chevalier, A. Gheerbrandt, *Dizionario dei Simboli.*
12. M. Gimbutas, *Il linguaggio della Dea.*
13. M. Eliade, *Trattato di storia delle religioni.*
14. M. Gimbutas, *Il linguaggio della Dea.*
15. E. Harding, *I misteri della donna.*
16. C. Pont-Humbert, *Dizionario dei simboli, dei riti e delle credenze.*
17. M. Eliade, *Trattato di storia delle religioni.*
18. M. Eliade, *Trattato di storia delle religioni.*

3.12

10 The Hands

The Hands

The women discover that the arms and hands can gracefully "frame" the movements of the body.

One of the goals I set for myself in my workshops is to help the woman appreciate the movements of the arms and hands and not to consider them less important than the dance's central movement of the hips. I like to begin lessons sitting on the floor, so that we can concentrate on the upper body and the breathing and become aware of the calmness that we can create when we find a connection between the two. We leave the usual, hectic rhythm of daily life outside the door.

Giving their full attention to the upper body, the women discover that the arms and hands can gracefully "frame" the movements of the body. They can also become the protagonists of the dance when we use the slow, sensual music of a *taksim* (musical improvisation with one instrument, usually flute or violin). Focusing their attention on the hands, they feel an incredible mobility in their fingers and they develop their sense of touch. While we dance, the palms and fingers wander through the air near the body, as if they are making a flower bloom with their caress. The hands can feel the heat that radiates from the skin and we begin to develop a kind of sensitivity that we are not in frequent contact with.

The hand has a magical value in this dance: it's the tool that forms the world of our spirit. It is the sensory medium through which we first understood the physical aspects of the world as children, and now as adults we sink ourselves into it and give ourselves back.[1] Through our hand gestures, we express our generosity as dancers. It's no coincidence that the first contact we usually make with people is done through the handshake, a moment in which we receive a lot of information about the other person, and in a certain way, we "mutually read each other," with the "people-sensing radar," the hand.[2]

The hand is like the eye in that is has the ability to let us "see" the world. The words "manifestation" and "manage" have the same root, which comes from the Latin word for hand manus. Something that is "manifest," can almost be touched; it is the physical representation of the brain's idea. In ancient times, the hand was seen as the external pendant of the human brain. This connection actually does have a scientific base, because it is now known that 60 percent of the brain's surface area corresponds to our ten fingers. Significantly enough, when we dance using the

The Ouled Nail *are very famous dancers who live in the Sahara desert in Algeria. They still dance in order to receive their dowries, and they use the Hand of Tanit as charms. This is similar to the Hand of Fatima, and is among the most well-known, magic talismans used in the Islamic world."*

hands in a coordinated way, we are stimulating the brain, because synchronized movements increase the blood levels in our brains by 5 to 15 percent.[3]

The symbol of the hand has an interesting connection with the arrow. It reminds us that the name of Chiton (Sagittarius), the figure represented by an arrow, is derived from the word for hand. In fact, the hand guides us; it brings us in a determined direction. In dance, it often happens that the hand orients the dancer's stare. Her eyes follow the path of her hands and the people in the audience then follow the dancer's stare.

The hand has an important feminine value, and in the past it was a regal emblem, the symbol of creative power and the power of the Goddess: the Hebrew word *iad*, means both hand and power.[4] "Isis, the left hand," was the mother's hand, and it protected humans. Even in ancient times, they painted pictures of hands on stone as a defense against natural disasters.

The hand as a symbol of stimulating force, the Goddess's energy, was called the *Pantea Hand*, the "Hand of all the Goddesses." It was often represented by magic symbols, animals, and the signs of the zodiac.[5] Later, it was adopted by the Islamic world as the *Khomsa*, which means "five fingers" in Arabic and is also known as "Fatima's hand."

Tanit's hand and the Khomsa ("five fingers" in Arabic) or Fatima's hand.

The hand is an invocation of protection and benediction. We see it in statues and depictions of holy people who offer up the palm of the hand sending a blessing. Our hands have incredible power. They can comfort, cure, and calm others down, for instance, when we quiet down a baby or place a hand on someone to reassure him or her. In belly dancing, we cannot ignore this power. Rather, we should include it as an important part of our body language: through our hand gestures, the poetry of the soul is revealed.

The movement of the hands in belly dancing

I n belly dancing, the movements that the hands trace in the air are expressive rather than narrative. For this reason, they are not given specific meanings as they are in the *mudra*, the solemn rituals transcending from Indian mysticism, which we also see in their dance. Instead, they transmit the spiritual energy of the dancer. The circular movement typical of belly dancing begins with the wrist and finishes with the fingers, drawing a continuous circle, fluid and cyclical, like the Life it represents.

Girls can begin to discover belly dancing's hand language at a very young age, along with its everyday, poetic significance. (My daughter, Martinica, while she dances at Omphalos).

Years ago, I decided to go completely on my own instinct and began explaining the subtle hand movements by basing them on different images that are traditionally feminine, movements that represent daily actions: painting the body with henna, combing the hair, sewing, weaving, playing an instrument, putting on make-up, bathing, floating, giving or getting a massage, getting dressed, taking care of the body (your own or others') etc.

Not only were the lessons more fun, but after I little while, I noticed that the women understood what technique to use with their hands, and the tiny little movements that they made gave the dance an incredible refinement and delicacy as it helped them create and choreograph. In this way, they were able to avoid the automatic, exaggerated hand movements that often occur and that take attention away from the other parts of the body that we might be focusing on at that moment.

In the Neolithic world, there were many hand actions used by women that made important inventions possible at that time and aided in the development of civilization: agriculture, weaving, sewing, spinning, ceramics, and gathering food, all of which required quick and agile fingers, preferably small-boned with articulate mobility instead of the more robust hand.[6]

During this long period, the main art form was ceramics and it was practiced by women who, using their agile and precise hands, produced for the first time a great abundance of circular designs. Their themes were not only natural, but also symbolic and cosmic.

The primordial female mystery, the foundation of belly dancing, is connected with the reality of daily life, "common" actions, and our interaction with nature. We see it in the archetypal activities that hid one entire specific perception of Life, a "guarded secret." For example, through the art of weaving and spinning, they transmitted their religious familiarity with the cycles of life, death, and beyond.[7] Belly dancing was originally in direct contact with daily activities, and therefore the archetypes and primordial mysteries. Dancing with our hands we feel this ancient knowledge come back to us

The Threads of Existence

I n many primitive traditions, weaving has a beautiful symbolism that represents the ability to create a life plan, to bring the threads together and form a harmonious design.[8] This action is expressed in the image of the Goddess: the "Lady of Fate," who creates human existence with her hands, the web of the Universe, the destiny of the world.

In many myths, "reality" is the work of the master weavers. All the activities like braiding, weaving, tying, and knotting come back into the universal feminine actions that determine Fate or Destiny. The Great Goddess, adorned with the moon and a lace shawl made of the nocturnal stars, weaves life, and therefore our destiny.[9] The woman herself, being a giver of life, is the great weaver- the "spider woman" who weaves a cosmic web that captures humans' destiny and takes it back at the end of time.

Because of this, spiders are often associated with women and female tasks. The female spider spins her web from nothing, directly from her body, and this is a fact that makes her a living symbol of inner creativity. The web also has a cosmic symbolism in that its threads are interconnected and interdependent just as humans are in their relationships with each other and with the universe.

> The woman herself, being a giver of life, is the great weaver- the "spider woman" who weaves a cosmic web that captures humans' destiny and takes it back at the end of time.

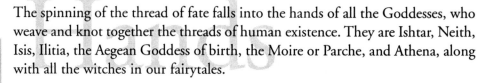

The spinning of the thread of fate falls into the hands of all the Goddesses, who weave and knot together the threads of human existence. They are Ishtar, Neith, Isis, Ilitia, the Aegean Goddess of birth, the Moire or Parche, and Athena, along with all the witches in our fairytales.

The spindle in the fairytale "Sleeping Beauty" is a symbol of destiny and negative magic influence, while for the lunar religions, the spindle that spins in a uniform circle was a positive symbol of eternal return. It represented the omnipotent character of destiny and the movement of Life and time, which manifested in the constant flow of birth to death to life.[10]

Knots are also essential elements in weaving, related to the symbol of the belt.

In the fairytale "Sleeping Beauty," a fairy godmother predicts the princess's death when she pricks her finger on the spindle. The act of spinning in this story is a symbol of destiny and negative magic influence.

They represent the fusion that keeps magical powers from escaping, and this presence is universal in talismans. In Russia, the wedding gowns have a belt braided with knots that is said to provide protection from the evil eye. Similarly, the Greeks and Romans used ornaments in the form of a braid, spiral, or knot that offered protection.[11] In the ancient Egyptian tradition, all knots possessed a sacred quality: Isis, the great sorceress, knew the science of knots and was able to tie and untie them.[12]

Later, the symbolism of interlocking threads and weaving became expressions of the sexual act, of two partners who get together and "weave" our existence.

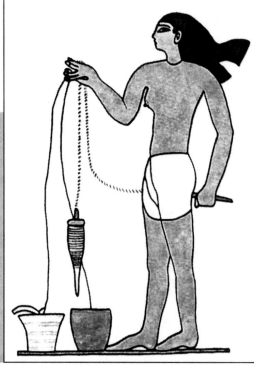

Nell'antichità il fuso era associato al fato e all'eterno ritorno, e perciò rappresentativo del principio femminile, della creatività e della continuazione della vita. Filatrice egizia.

Through this dance, we are invited to weave our own destinies, to create a thread starting at the center, and to spin a choreographic web of our knowledge that we can share with others. It's a calling for independence and self-awareness.

WORKS CITED IN CHAPTER 3.12

1. M. Mala, *Mani magiche.*
2. C. Pinkola Estés, *Donne che corrono coi lupi.*
3. M. Mala, *Mani magiche.*
4. J. Chevalier, A. Gheerbrandt, *Dizionario dei Simboli.*
5. B. Walker, *The Woman's Dictionary…*
6. J. Clottes, *La preistoria spiegata ai miei nipoti.*
7. C. Pinkola Estés, *Donne che corrono coi lupi.*
8. C. Risé e M. Paregger, *Donne selvatiche.*
9. E. Neumann, *La grande madre.*
10. J. Chevalier, A. Gheerbrandt, *Dizionario dei Simboli.*
11. C. Pont-Humbert, *Dizionario dei simboli…*
12. C. Jacq, *Il segreto dei geroglifici.*

3.13

Cymbals are helpful in expressing yourself, making your real voice be heard. With them we aim to enhance the hand work and invite the audience to appreciate it. Group exercises at IALS in Rome (photo: C. Ferrara)

11 The Cymbals' Dialogue

The Cymbals' Dialogue

One of the most satisfying skills for a dancer who is beginning to have a certain command of the belly dancing's language is being able to use the cymbals with intention. Right from her entrance, the dancer is energized by the powerful scenic presence the cymbals create. Their effect is prolonged during the choreography when she accentuates her movements with their sound, making sure that they become more visible to the spectators. At last, during the finale, she beats her feet to the rhythm of the music and closes the dance with vigor.

The cymbals lend us their voice to converse with the music- or with the musicians in the case of a live performance- through musical phrases and accents. The gestures can become a game of call and answer, which require the dancer to listen to the melody and rhythm, until the rhythm becomes interior. Then we are able to dance and play at the same time without losing the tempo, and we pause while using the cymbals, creating moments of silence within the music.

The cymbals are helpful in expressing yourself, making your true voice be heard, but also in listening to what is going on around you. They should be played using a dialogue, a give and take, an exchange. This exchange is not only done with the music, but also the body movements, intuition, the spectators, and whatever is happening around you. When I play the cymbals, I don't think about creating a monologue. What I mean is that if we start a rhythm and keep going with it, like horses racing round and round a track, it can be unpleasant for those who are listening. For this reason, I look for an effect when I use the cymbals. I look for something that "breathes," enhances the hand work, and invites the audience to appreciate it.

Usually when I teach the cymbals (a practice that is very useful, even for beginners, to understand the music in respect to the movement of the body), before explaining the various rhythms, I spend a good amount of time setting the scene: giving importance to the hands, moving them with the arms, becoming familiar with the space and understanding how to accentuate our movements. We practice movements feeling the weight and dimensions of the cymbals, which should be held and used in such a way that they make our dance more elegant, rather than weighing us down. With these preparations, moving the arms and hands through the air, you can also get over the fear of dropping them on the floor, something that shouldn't happen if the cymbals are adjusted properly with the elastics around the fingers. If it does

When selecting the right cymbals, it's good to listen to their vibration, touching the edges of the two disks together very delicately. The sound that emanates should be pleasant and should gradually become less intense. The disks with two parallel openings for the elastics are preferable (and not the ones with just one circular hole, as shown in the picture on the left), in this way, the elastic stays on the fingers better and provides more stability and control. (graphic: Simonetta Retica)

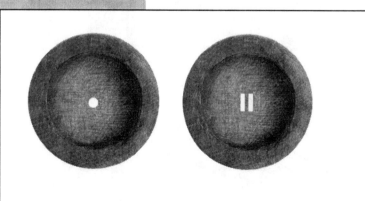

happen, that's okay, because experience comes from overcoming our difficulties and learning from our mistakes.

We then look at the correspondence between the movements and the sounds, which are very specific and harmoniously linked. It's a fun discovery if accompanied by the voice. Finally- and this is the most delicate phase- we play the cymbals and dance at the same time.

I encourage you not to slam the cymbals together, but to play them delicately, to understand their vibrations, and to do it assertively, giving a welcoming to this presence of sound, and to their message- the inner dialogue- which begins to come out through the dance.

The cymbals are helpful in expressing yourself, making your true voice be heard, but also in listening to what is going on around you: they should be played using a dialogue, a give and take, an exchange. This exchange is not only made with the music, but also the body movements, intuition, the spectators, and whatever is happening around you.

The Three-beat Rhythm

Interestingly enough, the rhythm that we base the use of the cymbals on has three beats: right, left, right, with the stress on the last beat. This is a very significant coincidence because, just as nature implements a three part structure, the three-beat rhythm reflects the time phases of every process: beginning, middle, and end; birth, life and death; past, present, and future. All of these sequences reflect the cyclical reality of Life, the essential feminine nature, cyclical, not linear time, a well-formed completeness. This circular reality is, therefore, revealed clearly in belly dancing through its movements and in the main rhythm that can be accompanied by the cymbals.

The Goddess's Sacred Instruments

In ancient times, the cymbals (also called *sagat, sunouj, zills,* and *zang*) were sacred instruments belonging to the Divine. In fact, their name is derived from the great Goddess Cybele, the "Mountain Mother." She is depicted as an older, well-endowed woman who carried grain on her head and keys in her hands, and was draped in cloth containing all the colors of the flowers that grew on the land she ruled over.[1]

Her cult was started in Anatolia, modern-day Turkey, and spread throughout the Mediterranean. She was very popular in Rome for many centuries, until her main temple was destroyed with the overtaking of Christianity and- a fact that is unack-

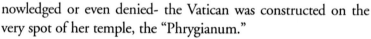

Cybele, pulled by lions. Rome, c. 2nd century B.C.

nowledged or even denied- the Vatican was constructed on the very spot of her temple, the "Phrygianum."

Cymbals have always been used everywhere in the Middle East and North Africa, from Persia, to Arabia, to Morocco. Cymbals from around 1000 B.C. were found in Babylonia and Iraq. In Egypt, they discovered a manuscript that turns out to be the contract for a dancer who used cymbals, and dates back to the first century before Christ. These instruments are also play a big part in a story of a boy who falls off a wall after climbing up it to watch a dancer play the cymbals.

They were also used in ancient Rome during the ritual worship of Bacchus (Dionysus). A type of cymbal, "castanets," were sometimes made of metal instead of wood. These instruments are used in Andalusia's sinuous dance, the Zambra mora. This hybrid dance of half belly dancing and half flamenco is performed by barefoot dancers, who don't use the "castanuelas" of the flamenco, but rather the same cymbals that we use.

WORK CITED IN CHAPTER 3.13

1. P. Monaghan, *Le donne nei miti e nelle leggende.*

The cymbals were used during the ritual worship of Bacchus (Dionysus), as we see in this scene. Villa dei Misteri, Pompei, Italy.

3.14

(photo: C. Ferrara).

12 The Water of Life

The Water of Life

«When you do dance, I wish you / A wave o'the sea,
that you might ever do / Nothing but that».

W. Shakespeare, The Winter's Tale

Sometimes while I'm improvising a dance and I don't feel very good about how it's turning out, I start working with the symbol of water, which helps me find my center and stabilize my body. Through the movements of the dance, I can float and flow through the space around me. Little by little, I feel calmer and more focused. My movements are intensified and everything becomes easier and more enjoyable.

Water is an image that I use in my lessons, because it helps the women find the fluidity to go from one move to another and prolong them in a graceful way, almost as if they want to stay behind the music. This gives the idea that the dance is elastic and is suspended in time. It's hard to put into words! But the symbol of water helps me a great deal, because it provides a certain sensation that everyone knows and everyone can invoke when necessary.

When it starts to get hot around June, I propose a lesson in the water, in our pool at Omphalos. What better way to learn about the dance's fluidity! At first none of the dancers really expect to have this kind of lesson, since it seems a little strange, but everyone ends up bringing their bathing suits willingly because it sounds like fun. In fact, these water lessons have become a special treat.

Everyone learns well in the water. Usually we do a warm up, with one hand on the side of the pool, using it as a dance bar. We make circular movements with each part of the body, keeping them underwater so that we can feel the resistance. The body moves slowly and, because of the water's weight and opposition, the movement is pleasantly smooth and continuous. The arms tend to elongate and move gracefully, and even when working with another area of the body, they help maintain good posture. The lesson is very relaxing and allows us to understand how to do the more difficult steps, such as moving to the side through undulations- also called the camel- a move that has many variations. The version I like the best is a little bit hard to execute. It begins by bringing the chest up, while the weight of the body is simultaneously carried forward and then backward as the belly contracts.

The water is a useful tool because it gives the body support, but also moves with it. Holding some of the body's weight, it helps us move gradually and gently. It's impossible to make sudden, random movements in the water, so this is a good lesson on the quality of movement we are aiming for in the dance.

Dancing then becomes more of a sensory experience for the women, and when we go back to dancing "on dry land," we are full of emotion, because the water makes us feel *wrapped up*, completely *embraced*.

> The water is a useful tool because it gives the body support, but also moves with it. Holding some of the body's weight, it helps us move gradually and gently. It's impossible to make sudden, random movements in the water, so this is a good lesson on the quality of movement we are aiming for in the dance.

In it, we lose our sense of gravity; we feel ethereal. We can dance with a continuous flow. It requires us to let it all go, instead of wanting to control everything, even when we dance.

In the water, you learn to go with the flow, literally, and to get over the fear of dancing with Life, with whatever is happening around you at that moment. When you synchronize yourself with the water, there is a unity in the rhythm, and it seems like the music and your dance become one.

In the water, you learn to go with the flow, literally, and to get over the fear of dancing with Life, with whatever is happening around you at that moment.

Water is the element that brings the feminine principle of excellence to life. Many ancient Goddesses were associated with the water. It was said that Aphrodite was born from the cosmic ocean, and for this reason was called "anadiomene," or "from the sea." Ashera was known as the "Lady of the Ocean," and Ishtar was the "Queen of the Water." Aphrodite in her seashell. Hermitage Museum.

The Water of Life

But water is a primordial substance. The land we live on is in the middle of water, the human body is three-fourths water, and all of it's functions are regulated by water. It's so important that it was used therapeutically as one of the first medicines in ancient times.

Working with water reminds you how important this element is in our lives, even though it's something we usually take for granted- as long as it's there when you turn on the faucet! But water is a primordial substance. The land we live on is in the middle of water, the human body is three-fourths water, and all of it's functions are regulated by water. It's so important that it was used therapeutically as one of the first medicines in ancient times.

Dancing through the water I discovered that I had a special relationship with it, because its symbolism is closely connected to the origins of life, birth, and creativity. All of the major civilizations in history considered water to be the essential, cosmic element and a sacred, mythological element in the stories of Creation. The primordial water was linked to original chaos, when all of the elements were mixed together in one homogenous mass before life came out of it.

This cosmology is not just the primitive view on life; it is also backed up by scientific theories on the "primordial sludge," the material in which molecules first developed the ability to replicate themselves and produce new life forms.[1]

Originally, the kingdom of the Goddess was the mythical aquatic sphere. Aphrodite was born from the cosmic ocean; Ashera ,the Goddess of Canaan, was called the "Lady of the Ocean;" in Egypt, Ishtar was the "Queen of the Water," and Isis was said to be born from humidity.

Water holds the voice of the *Primordial Mother* since it is the universal womb. Every life began in liquid, which was actually very similar to the chemical composition of the ancient seas. Water is identified with the Goddess's cosmic belly, "the deep," from which mankind sprung in many of the myths of Creation. This symbol's feminine backdrop, which the ancients were completely aware of, is evident in many myths. For the Egyptians, it was Maa, or the goddess Temu who produced the first elements of existence, Water, Darkness, Night, and Eternity.

Ishtar, found in the Palazzo di Mari, 17ᵗʰ century B.C., represented as a Goddess with a vase-belly, a symbolic message that abundance and prosperity flowed from this place.

Temu became the Babylonian Goddess Tiamat, and also Tehom for the Jews. She is "the abyss" mentioned in Genesis 1:2, a symbolic representation of chaos, the bottomless pit of primordial water. The echo of the ancient cosmology that saw water as the spring of life, comparable to the mother, emerges in our modern day languages. For example, the French words for sea, mere, and mother, mer, are almost identical.

In Egyptian mythology, the luminous sky was the stretching body of the Goddess Nut. She extended her arms in a gesture of protection and nourished the land with her breastmilk, "the water of life."

In the Hebrew letter mem, we can also see the aspects of the symbol that represent sensitive water, mother and womb, source of all things, the manifestation of the sacred. As a reproductive act of renewal, birth requires a rebirth to fulfill its true meaning, as in the immersion rites of purification and regeneration. The holy bath, a very ancient ritual, was commonly practiced in the worship of the Goddesses of fertility and agriculture. It symbolized a return to the mysterious uterus, the ultimate vital water of Divinity.[2]

Up until the present day, the baptismal immersion has maintained its ritual meaning of transformation and return to the origin, as a mystic act of rebirth.[3] The worshiping of water is an instinctive devotion to the primordial element. This was brought to life in the "worship of the fountains," as well, which are still thought to be sources of life and renewal and have always been sought out by pilgrims.

The historical springs are associated with the Goddesses and nymphs of certain rivers, fountains, and wells. It was thought that all you had to do was take a drink, or dip part of the body in these special waters to be able to conceive a child, a belief based on the faith in water's power to give life. For the Greeks, water was a purifying spring of life which contained the elements of origin. Because of this, it was connected to marriage practices, in particular, the bride's bath, which required her to go to the local river and splash herself with water while saying a prayer asking to be blessed with children.[4]

The worshiping of water as a fertilizing element was based on the archaic belief that it had reproductive powers, and this concept is so widespread that it extends from the Neolithic era to present day. As the universal womb, the properties of water are similar to the vital fluids of the female body: blood, amnio-

The Water of Life

The ocean, as "primordial sludge" is comparable to the unborn child's "private ocean."

tic fluid, and milk. Aside from these symbols, water has also taken on different symbols of fertility, which are the origins and vehicles of life: the moon, the belly, and the snake, all interlocked in a rhythmic cosmology.

The ocean, as "primordial sludge" corresponds to the amniotic fluid that gave origin to human life and it's comparable to the unborn child's "private ocean." Water holds, nourishes, transforms, and rocks the baby. Every living creature develops and preserves its existence through water, the earth's milk. Water also symbolically belongs to the breast, since milk, "the water of life," springs forth in the same way. The celestial figure of the ancient Egyptian Goddess Nut represented femininity, and her breast nourished the land with its rain-milk, and her uterus, like a vase of birth broken to pieces, overflowed with water.

The feminine aspect of water is evident in the scenes on Neolithic vases, where water was represented by the symbol "VVV," the oldest Egyptian hieroglyph for flowing water. This sign also represented the woman, honoring her as a fresh water spring. In the same Egyptian cosmology, the primordial water of creation is connected to the symbol of the snake, as a creature coiled up in spirals, born out of the primordial ocean. We can find a similar idea in the myth of the water dance done by the Goddess Eurinome: the mother of all things rose up from chaos, and with a powerful dance on top of the waves, she separated sea from sky and created the snake, Ophione, out of the North wind.

Water and menstrual blood are two organic elements connected to the matriarchal symbolism of life. The symbol of water contains that of menstrual blood, which is then in turn connected to the moon. The menstrual cycle and the ocean's tides are both regulated by the changing phases of the moon.

The cosmic symbolism of reproduction, tied to the rhythms of the Moon, Water, and Woman, have given the process of life a feminine, cyclical structure. For this reason the symbols for the Moon, Water, and Woman have been perceived as both the human and cosmic circuit of fertility since prehistoric times.

It's interesting to note that water has masculine as well as feminine characteristics, in that it was seen as both the male who fertilized, and the female who gave birth. The water coming down in the form of rain was considered to be the male fertilizer of the land, while the original water rising from the land at dawn was considered to be female. The land, in this case, was associated with the moon as a symbol of perfect fertility, as the "pregnant land," from which water rose up. It was completely fertile and allowed germination to occur.

WORKS CITED IN CHAPTER 3.14

1. A. Stevens, *Il filo di Arianna.*
2. M. Eliade, *Trattato di storia delle religioni.*
3. E. Neumann, *La grande madre.*
4. I. Della Portella, *Roma sotterranea.*

3.15

(photo: C. Ferrara).

The 13 Eyes
The Stare's Eloquence

The Eyes

I In the Middle East, the power of the stare as a symbol of seduction is very tangible, as the result of an ancient tradition that has placed a lot of importance on eye contact. For the ancient Egyptians, the eye was a fundamental symbol, both magical and religious, which represented the regal authority of fire. Like fire, the eye shines, glazes over, illuminates, and burns.

The depiction of the eye lined in black had the widespread function as an amulet (Udiat), and was used for protection in the niches next to the front doors of houses, in tombs, and in works of art.

The eyes also had a cosmic significance because the sun and the moon were said to be the eyes of Horus (son and lover of Isis). The Egyptians called the moon "the Eye of Horus," but even before this, the symbol was an attribute of the goddess of truth, Maat, whose name is derived from the verb, "to see."[1]

The Eye of Horus, cosmic symbol of the moon, identified with fire itself. Symbol of vigilance, and the need to keep your eyes open, in the continuation of eternity.

This concentration on the stare is also the result of a traditional way of dressing in the Middle East, which, covering the body, emphasizes the face and in particular the eyes. At this point they have become "the epicenter, the essential fulcrum of seduction."[2] Anyone who has had the opportunity to observe a woman dressed in this way can attest to the fact that the eloquence of her eyes makes her stare more expressive. She is even more accustomed to using her eyes in daily life than a woman who doesn't cover her face. In the Arabic lyric poetry, and in *A Thousand and One Nights* (mistakenly called *Arabian Nights*), it's not rare to hear verses that celebrate the eyes: «Heavy stare full of anticipation / like the stare that a sick man directs / at his visitor.[3].

But the eyebrows also play an important part in the game and are sometimes described as the "cliffs of desirous eyes" and the eyelashes also have a role, batting to the same rhythm that many hearts have fallen in love to.

But the eyebrows also play an important part in the game and are sometimes described as the "cliffs of desirous eyes" and the eyelashes also have a role, batting to the same rhythm that many hearts have fallen in love to. And so, it is completely natural that dancers in the Middle East are used to putting a lot of emphasis on the eyes in their shows, using a dynamic language that includes the eyebrows and uses the hands to frame the face, either strengthening or hiding the stare.

This stare that seems to cut through the air, has more weight and is more expressive than words. It inspired me not to take the eyes for granted, but to see them as an interesting element in the dance. Especially for those of us who are not used to using them in such an intense way as the Middle Eastern women do. Our stare is much more casual. We are accustomed to using it as an automatic function, like breathing. When we wake up in the morning, the first thing we do is open our eyes and look around, and as the day unravels, our gaze comes with us and we don't think much of it. When we dance, we look inside ourselves, sometimes we look at the ground. But we use our eyes. It doesn't seem as though we have to work on the eyes as much as other parts of the body.

So it doesn't surprise me in the least when I propose a seminar on "the eloquence of the stare in belly dancing," and the women respond, "But are we going to dance? ….I thought I was already using my eyes when I danced!" Although many women are curious, some think that there are more important aspects of belly dancing to learn.

My question to them is, "*How* do we use our eyes?"

Is it a generic stare, or are we really *aware*? And that's my point.

That's one of my favorite challenges: choosing a theme that is often overlooked with the intention of giving it a new light in our dance.

Is it a generic stare, or are we really aware?

Seeing and being seen

A woman who starts belly dancing can progress until she knows her body well, overcomes her shyness, and internalizes her dance with more intensity if she uses the stare effectively. She has to be taught from the beginning to not always direct it at the mirror, but to focus the stare on her body and to feel the space around her.

However, a dancer with more expertise who works in public, finds herself dealing with the stare of others focused on her, and at the same time, with the need to "look at everyone," which is surely a talent refined by an intentional stare. This will help her use her eyes in a way that adds something to the dance, both as a tool to emphasize her movements and a window to her emotions, to her interior world.

Sometimes the challenge of performing in front of others makes the stare become generic: a little here a little there. You don't really focus because you haven't developed the ability to direct the stare with awareness. Or the opposite can be true, that a dancer constantly focuses her eyes on the audience trying to use her stare to *control* their reactions. She dances with the goal of accomplishing something, and getting results becomes her most important goal. So she concentrates more on the *effect* that her choreography has on others rather than the *pleasure* she can experience and share with others.

When focusing on the results, the dancer's inner dialogue is usually full of "have to's": I have to be happy because the music is upbeat, I have to involve the audience, I have to keep an eye on the time, I have to smile, and so on. As a con-

…a dancer with more expertise finds herself dealing with the need to look at everyone…

sequence, the emotions are "forced." The mouth is forced into a smile and she looks around in a predisposed way. Even her feelings have already been decided upon. We are not ourselves anymore, and it's not possible to get much personal satisfaction from this type of work.

At this point, someone should remind me that dancers can find many difficulties in the places where belly dancing is usually presented. Of course, I know that not all venues will offer the right atmosphere for quality artistic work, and not all of the people in the audience will look for a profound meaning in the dance, but I think it's important to dance for those who might appreciate this art: we should give the "gift" to those people. Whoever loves this dance and dedicates herself to it with passion and devotion, knows that it hides a deep message. When I dance with intention, "someone" will understand it. I definitely have to force myself to be picky about where I dance, agreeing to work only in places that respect me as a person, as a woman, and as a dancer.

An aspect that carries a lot of weight is the visual impact we have and how we are perceived in different settings: our costumes and make-up are very important and reflect what we want to present through belly dancing.

An aspect that carries a lot of weight is the visual impact we have and how we are perceived in different settings: our costumes and make-up are very important and reflect what we want to present through belly dancing.

The Message we Send through How we Look: costume and make-up

A face made-up delicately and artfully can accentuate the expression of our eyes, giving the face life and color. Sometimes it can even have a dramatic, theatrical effect that helps us create the character we are trying to interpret. When dancers ask me for advice on these matters, I suggest that they put their make-up on carefully, blending the colors well, and taking into account their distance away from the audience. If the people are far away, or if they'll be dancing on stage under the lights, the make-up should be heavier, where if they are in a more intimate, familiar atmosphere, it should be lighter and well-blended to avoid looking too fake or "plastic." It could help to take a quick course in make-up to learn the tricks of the trade, so that you can put it on well and quickly.

And what about the message we send through our costumes?

Many women manage to get really creative in their use of fabric and different materials to create an original costume. Others prefer to go with one of the "classical" two-piece costumes made in different Middle Eastern countries. Whether you choose an original costume or a typical one, it should be comfortable (even if it's heavy). A good costume gives us grace and makes us feel beautiful and special.

When trying different costumes on, you should dance a little bit to test it out. Raise your arms, spin, do a shimmy, and undulate the body to see how you feel in it. Just as when you're buying a nice pair of shoes, you stand up and walk around a little, to choose a belly dancing costume, you need to see it in action. Sometimes the dancers ask me how to choose a costume that's not "too much," that's still sensual without being risqué. Obviously, every woman has her own tastes. I personally find it enjoyable to put on a costume that allows people to see me in a subtle, sensual way, but I don't choose anything that reduces my body or my presence in front of an audience to a sex object. It's a little like how I see the dance itself: our more sensual movements are delicately "suggestive." In the same way, our most sensual costumes can be suggestive but still leave something to the imagination. A well-made costume helps me give the dance flight, in all aspects, and doesn't limit it just to the erotic aspect. Alright, now that I've given my two cents on the external aspect, I'd like to get back to the emotional aspect of the dance: Are we ready to dance in front of others?

Just like when you're buying a nice pair of shoes and you stand up and walk around a little, to choose a belly dancing costume, you need to see it in action.

Taking Risks in front of an Audience

I don't think it's easy to dance in front of and look out at an audience, no matter how small the group is. Actually, sometimes a small group of people we know can cause more problems for us than an audience of 1000 strangers. It takes a lot of courage to perform for people and to really experience the dance as we feel it. There are many risks: we could fail to entertain them, be criticized, be accused. Some people might attack us with dirty looks, others might get up and leave, some might fall asleep, and others might whisper bad things about our performances, or like in the cartoons, they might throw tomatoes at us! An artist always takes risks; it would certainly be easier to remain anonymous, follow others, and conform to general rules. But art is taking risks. It asks for a subjective point of view, not a unanimous group opinion.

Many of the problems that arise in this situation come from the fact that we feel like others are judging us. Sometimes this seems to be the hardest thing for dan-

The

Maria dressed in blue, with the audience after a show in Turku, Finland.

cers. However, in my experience, the biggest difficulty we really have comes from being judged by the critic inside of us, who lashes out a worse punishment than a front row full of averse critics. It's hard to dance and keep eye contact with the others without succumbing to their opinions, but it's even harder to dance in front of an audience and not be our own worst critics!

With time and constant work, this negative voice that always finds our flaws should become quieter and eventually fade away, giving precedence to the interior voice that encourages us and focuses on the positive and most satisfying things that we've accomplished. It gives us support with a "Bravo, nice job!"

To grow in this dance we have to learn to give priority to the inner voice that doesn't judge us, but accepts all the emotions that come to the surface.

To grow in this dance we have to learn to give priority to the inner voice that doesn't judge us, but accepts all the emotions that come to the surface. Sometimes we have the idea that belly dancing is "sparkling," happy, festive. It is true that it's also these things, but it shouldn't be limited to just the bright side of life. Through the dance we express our inner world, with all its colorful emotions. We show happiness, softness, and passion, but also pain, sadness, and anger, which have their own repercussions in the way we use our stare.

We become more familiar with this art to find depth in our lives; I'm convinced of this, even in the cases of people who start dancing just to "get a little exercise."

The dance is like life, it requires us to express ourselves for who we are, to live genuinely, not to deny our emotions in front of others, and to be positive when we present something that we believe in. I don't think I'm exaggerating when I say that it's a heroic attitude. On this dancing journey, we shouldn't ignore the fact that we feel afraid, or embarrassed, feelings that the body shows through shortness of breath, wobbly legs, a racing heart, dry lips, etc. These are part of the package for those who work in the world of entertainment; they're there. Forever. Maybe less today or tomorrow. But they are a part of what can happen when we go in front of a group. And that's okay.

I can also feel vulnerable. However, it wouldn't be unheard of for the audience watching me to appreciate the courage of my work, and the difficulty that I find and try to overcome, *in front of them.*

I think these people are there to accompany me on my journey, which is what life resembles. It's full of unexpected danger. They come to see our show, and maybe even to find something more in their lives, to reflect on what we do, to dream or to believe. If that weren't the truth, then why do people sometimes cry when they watch a dance that pulls them in completely?

I don't think our responsibility to the audience is to please them or seduce them, or keep them awake, or not to offend them, even if they pay to get in. It's to offer our art in the most authentic way possible. Then we can let every person think what they want to. They can have their own reactions, they can appreciate it or not.

In any case, it's not very likely that a dance really lived on the inside doesn't have a positive impact. But you never know! We also have to accept that our work might not be for everyone.

The Stare's Anchors

During our lessons, I ask the dancers to start from where we are: to slowly feel the breathing which, along with the sensations that the music evokes, the people we have in front of us, and the movements that happen step by step, ensures that the dance will transform and come to life in a different way every time.

To be at ease while we work and give our inner beings room to express themselves, we have to "lower our anchors"- this is indispensable during the moments of nervousness and fear. It doesn't have so much to do with our technical skill, but more with our ability to feel the *calm, deep breathing,* and with the ability to intentionally direct the stare to a single point- the *ability to set fire*, to spark. And we do this with the eyes.

To be at ease while we work and give our inner beings room to express themselves, we have to "lower our anchors."

One very enjoyable and unexpected aspect of this approach to the stare, is that we invade other areas. The first and foremost is acting, because the stare has to do with our stage presence, our charisma. For this reason, I often use acting exercises, which help me watch others and be watched without losing myself.

Then there is also the field of psychology, because with a stare we can read the interior life of another person, and having someone stare at us makes many barriers and fears rise up.

Still another area we can look to is yoga, which teaches us to center ourselves and listen to our breathing through *pranayama*. It helps us look around with awareness.

Right from the beginning of the exercise, we realize how hard it is to look someone in the eyes and not have a defensive attitude that blocks our breathing. When we block our breathing, we're trying to protect ourselves and block the "uncomfortable" emotions, which are the ones that come out most easily when we are being watched by a group, or when we look someone in the eyes: fear, insecurity, embarrassment, anger, sadness. Thus, if I'm looking for eloquence in the stare, it's helpful and necessary to work on breathing during dance practice.

"Dancing: seeing and being seen," an exercise with one of the groups at IALS, Rome, (photo: Maristella).

The Intuition Refined by the Stare

The eyes are springs of intuition, symbols of light, fertility, and knowledge. They concern the spirituality of the body and are, therefore, the tools of our interior world.[4] This intuition, which sees the source of life in the eye's language, is prehistoric and was already present in the Paleolithic era.[5] In this period, there was a divine, sacred tone brought to the eyes and the stare, because just like the other openings of the body, the eyes were presented as places of exchange between the internal and external, and for this, as the moist, feminine source of Life.[6]

When I work with the eyes and scrutinize my dance space, or lay my eyes on my own hips, I increase my intuition. *I have more to offer because I can really feel my surroundings and everything that lives inside of me.*

Through my stare, I can also "read" the people around me.

When the message of the dance is fully understood, we don't feel like the stares are trying to invade us, to take possession of our bodies, to refuse our space. They are stares that don't keep their distance in a detached or judgmental way, but instead, they gather up our dance like a gift that is offered from the heart.

A big part of our stage *presence* depends on the eyes. As mirrors of the soul, the eyes are also windows into the inner lives of our bodies. With the eloquence of their language, we add something unexpected and poetic to the dance.

Through the eyes we can literally get closer to people; we have an impact on the person looking at us. We can lightly graze them, charm them, or strike them with our different types of stares. Therefore, the eyes are an integral part of body movement, just like a movement of the hips, a spin with the veil, or a deep breath. Refining the stare is just as important as working on the technique of the steps in the dance studio. When we focus our eyes well, the dance seems to become easier, more centered. We know what to do when we're in front of others: when to give and when to make a private space for ourselves. We know how to smoothly use the stare to create a bridge that facilitates contact with others, exploring the different possibilities within the space and the body, matching it all to the music, looking at people directly, and so forth.

Now I would like to propose a game for you to work on the different possibilities offered by belly dancing's use of the eyes. I'm giving you this exercise not as a recipe, but as a starting point to develop this intentional stare. It's good to keep in mind that when we dance in public, the "guidelines" of staring are different from those of everyday life. We can get away with a little more, for example, staring at someone for a long time, or looking away from them all of a sudden, closing the eyes half-way, or shooting a glance like an arrow. The important thing is that we're aware of its power, and that we aren't afraid to use it. It's part of life and part of the heart's communication. It's also helpful to keep in mind the personal preferences we have for one type of look over another, but it's good to use all of them in a dance and to observe the reactions of both ourselves and those around us.

> Through my stare, I can also "read" the people around me.

> When we focus our eyes well, the dance seems to become easier, more centered.

The Game of Seven Stares

"Open your eyes and use your imagination in your dance space," Omphalos Theater.

The greeting stare

1. When I enter the room covered by a veil, I arouse an air of mystery. I don't start to dance yet; this is just an introduction. The look I give to the people is brief and calm. It's just enough to "greet" them, get a feeling for the atmosphere at that particular moment, understand my own state of mind, find my breath, and decide how I want to use my dance space. It creates mystery and anticipation. Later, when the real dancing starts, I alternate between glances at the audience, the area around me, and my own body. I don't let my eyes wander around randomly; I use them with intention, as if they were a major part of the body, like an arm or a leg.

The area stare

2. I open up the dance's stare and use my imagination in the area around me and above me. I don't make direct eye contact with the people. I concentrate on the dance space, spreading my body all around as if I could reach the furthest points of the room.

The pause and stare

3. This is a brief look in the eye, similar to what a public speaker does when pausing at a comma or giving emphasis to a point. In this way, I move around

the area, dancing and looking; I can see how everything's going. It helps keep me in contact with the audience, understand their mood, and let their feedback inspire my creativity.

4. Even if I'm looking directly at someone, my eyes, my body, and sometimes even my head are not positioned to face the person directly, but instead, on the diagonal, with a three-quarters stare. Another way is to direct the stare at someone, but use the hands as a veil, keeping them near the eyes so that they cover part of the face. This type of stare is good for "diluting" the dance's content, which otherwise could become too intense or risqué with a centered, direct stare. It can be used to suggest, to create mystery. I can look at people for a long time without my eyes becoming too invasive or my dance misunderstood.

The indirect stare

5. This is when I turn my back to the audience, or I cover my face completely with my hands. I use it to create a private little space in front of a group, where it's easier for me to internalize my thoughts, or stay "by myself" for a couple of seconds. I can also choose not to look at anyone, but to focus on my body instead, as I often do with the slow music of a *taksim*. In this way, I bring the group's attention to whatever I'm doing, to the more subtle moves, such as the shimmy. I give myself room to create an interior gaze. I can transmit profound, sensual content with grace and power. If I then bring my attention back to the exterior, it creates a nice balance of opposites.

The un-stare

6. This is when I strike someone or something with my stare and set that point on fire. All of the body movements and, naturally, the eyes, are directed at that one point. This works when you want to give special attention to someone or be playful, for example, if you're dancing at a birthday party. Or if you want to place importance on an object, such as the veil, or a determined point in the dance space.

The sharp stare

7. When I want to put emphasis on a movement, or make something more visible, I fix my eyes on a specific point for just a moment. This brings the audience's attention to that point. I pause for a second, which is actually very effective and charged with energy. I use this move to illustrate a strong musical accent, for example, when I focus on my hip as it stresses the last beat of music. It requires a good knowledge of the technique and music, so that you can coordinate everything. It's helpful in creating dramatic tension. This stare is a self-affirmation; I use it when I'm not looking for excuses or permission. Usually when I use it at the end of a dance, I call it the final fixed stare, because it goes along with the last movement that I use to close the dance.

The fixed stare

WORKS CITED IN CHAPTER 3.15

1. B. Walker, *The woman's Dictionary of Symbols and Sacred Objects.*
2. M. Chebel, *Il libro delle seduzioni.*
3. M. Chebel, *Il libro delle seduzioni.*
4. A. Lowen, *La spiritualità del corpo.*
5. M. Gimbutas, *Il linguaggio della Dea.*
6. E. Neumann, *La grande madre.*

Salome painted by Moreau,
"The Apparition."
Paris, Louvre.

The Invisible Dance
The Symbolism
of the Veil

The Veil

> «Salome, Salome dance for me. I pray thee dance for me. I am sad to-night.... Therefore dance for me, dance for me Salome, I beseech thee. If thou dancest for me thou mayest ask of me what thou wilt, and I will give it thee. Yes, dance for me, Salome, and whatsoever thou shalt ask of me I will give it thee, even unto the half of my kingdom».
>
> Herod in Oscar Wilde's *Salome*.

"And Salome danced the dance of the seven veils," wrote Oscar Wilde in 1893 when he gave the character Salome* an erotic, gyrating theatrical dance. During the puritanical climate of that era, this scene made the theaters showing the opera close down on more than one occasion. However, it then transformed into a huge success and paved the way for the "salomania" (the fashion trend of Salome's style). From that point on, "the dance of seven veils," a dance of seduction and revenge inspired by the character of Salome, continued to be performed in theaters and immortalized in painting, sculpture, music, and choreography. Even today it plays a part in the collective vision of both the Veil dance and belly dance.

But was it with "the dance of the seven veils" that the sixteen-year-old Salome made John the Baptist lose his head...literally? Reading the historical sources found in the New Testament (*Matthew* 14:3-11 and *Mark* 6:17-22) we find that Salome is not mentioned by name. They speak of "the daughter of Herodias" and there is no mention of a veiled dance, in that we don't know what kind of dancing she did or what type of costume she wore. It just tells us that "she danced." The story is usually told in this way: Herodias, Salome's mother, wanted to get revenge on John the Baptist, who had slandered her and publicly accused her of an illegal marriage to Herod, due to their blood relation, because she was his niece. Taking advantage of the occasion of the king's birthday party, Herodias had her daughter Salome dance for him. She danced with such skill that, as her reward, Herod offered to grant her any wish. Under her mother's pressure, she asked for the head of John the Baptist, who was already in prison at the time. The king begged her to ask for something else, but Salome wouldn't budge and in the end, Herod was forced to give the order and have John the Baptist beheaded. He presented the head to Salome on a platter, which she then brought to her mother.

Now I would like to clear up a very common misconception: the Veil dance did not come from Salome's erotic dance of revenge. This type of dance was only used to

---

* It was during the same year that "Little Egypt" introduced belly dancing to the States at the World Fair in Chicago. Some scholars think that Oscar Wilde was inspired by the dance of the seven veils described by Pierre Louys in his book of erotic poems, *The Song of Bilitis*.

At the beginning of the 1900s the woman was represented with characteristic of the "femme fatale," dangerous and sensual, inspired by the Western vision of the Orient.
Theda Bara as the seductress in Cleopatra, 1917.

make a better theatrical show for the character created by Wilde at the end of the 19th century. This performance then inspired the opera Salome composed by Richard Strauss in 1905, which dedicated nine long minutes to the "dance of the seven veils." These two operas clearly defined the character of Salome for future generations and served as examples for other "women of sin," such as Mata Hari and Cleopatra.[1]

Clearing up this common misconception, we aren't forced to think of the Veil dance as an instrument in the expression of the manipulative, destructive spirit of the "femme fatale." This was an image conjured up from the ideas, fears and fantasies, men had around the end of the 1800s. This figure of the erotic woman was the result of an obsession with the Orient at the time. But we can look for other sources of its inspiration that are more constructive.

The next step would be to ask ourselves: If it wasn't inspired by the Biblical dance of Salome, where does this Veil dance we see performed by belly dancers come from?

The Veil dance is a very ancient art, but the version we see performed today was developed with renewed strength in the 1900s. Before getting into its ancient origins, I'd like to distinguish between the two different styles of Veil dance that we see performed today and that are relatively new: the Egyptian style and the American style.

In the Egyptian style, the dancer enters with the veil in her hands and not attached as a tunic or a part of her costume. This dance is not practiced in an of itself, because in the cultural context of the Middle East, a real veil dance would be considered "out of place" by the dancers and the audience. I won't talk about the significance of the Islamic veil in this section*- let's just say that the specific meaning of the veil in the Middle East, which is a part of their clothing, or in any case, their cultural identity, makes sure that the veiled woman remains "inside" even when she's "outside." This attribute makes the game of covering and uncovering the body with fabric while you dance seem more like undignified behavior than an artistic, sensual, elaborate style of dance.

> The veiled dance is a very ancient art, but the version we see performed today was developed with renewed strength in the 1900s.

---

*There are many interesting sources on this topic including F. Mernissi, *Beyond the Veil*.

The Invisible Dance. The Symbolism of the Veil

187

The Veil

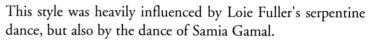

In the Egyptian style the dancer doesn't use the veil as a part of her costume. Usually, she just enters holding it in her hand and, after a brief introduction and a few dance moves, she stops using the veil and sets it aside to go on with the belly dancing.

The other style is a mix of different veil dance traditions, because it has been influenced by many cultures; however, it was developed primarily in the United States.

This style was heavily influenced by Loie Fuller's serpentine dance, but also by the dance of Samia Gamal.
Gamal was a famous Egyptian dancer who, in the Hollywood films of the 1940s, began to dance with a veil to add something extra to her presence on screen.
This curious idea was suggested to her by her Russian teacher, the dancer Ivanova, who had been inspired by Azerbaijan's dances in Caucasus.

The Veil dance continued to grow in the US until it became an art unto itself, finally coming down to us with precise technique and a specific language formed by many different moves.
In this style, the dancer usually enters with the veil attached to her costume, either as a tunic or wrapped around her. Then as she is dancing and spinning around fluidly, she removes the veil at the end of the first section of music. Only at this moment does the real Veil dance begin. She uses many different moves that are all intertwined with one another and inspired by the artist's creativity.

During the dance, the veil could be seen as a frame that makes the movements of the center of the body stand out. But it could also be used as a sail, a cloud, a dance partner, and many other things, until the dancer sets it aside to continue with the musical piece that follows.

Really, for every person, for every dancer, the veil has a different significance. It's a symbol that can express many ideas. But every one of us inevitably seeks a certain quality in the veil dance, an individual spirit.

Samia Gamal, famous Egyptian dancer with grace and style, who also had training in classical dance. She worked in Hollywood during the 40s, where she used the veil in her dancing.

Poster of Loie Fuller from 1898. She was a pioneer of modern dance and inspired the veiled dance. She took great pride in her art and watched over it with care, using different seamstresses to make her veils so that no one would discover the secret. She inspired painters, and sculptors of the Art Nouveau: Toulouse-Lautrec, Rodin, Bradley.

Poster of Loie Fuller from 1898. She was a pioneer of modern dance and inspired the veiled dance. She took great pride in her art and watched over it with care, using different seamstresses to make her veils so that no one would discover the secret. She inspired painters, and sculptors of the Art Nouveau: Toulouse-Lautrec, Rodin, Bradley.

Veiling and unveiling in the Veil Dance

In regards to every dancer's individual preferences, it should be up to her to decide the style that fits her best, but also the right moment to use this kind of dance. It requires a period of inner calmness and concentration, and can therefore be done in the middle of a dance and not necessarily at the beginning as described before. I have observed that, despite the style of veil dance chosen, when the piece is danced with creativity and life, the dancers always describe the veil as something more than a casual "accessory." They refer to the veil as if it were a living thing, something very important to them: "a dance partner," "my wings," "my soul," "an anchor that gives me security," "a sigh." As a tool of self-awareness: "it helps me see the music and the space," "it invites me to dance slowly and helps me overcome my difficulties," "it represents the things I don't know about myself," "I can simply play with it, as if I were a child again." Finally, as a spiritual aid: "it has a sacred presence," "it is a light, ethereal presence," "it has a secret soul," "it's translucent and pure," and many other affirmations that give it an emotional quality that we can't ignore.

Part of the veil's charm, I think, is that it makes us more independent. Even though it appears to be covering the body up and hiding us, in reality, we are free to choose when and how we want to reveal ourselves. It's not a veil we are forced to wear; we are the ones to decide how to play with it, how to express ourselves through it, or how to look for privacy under its wings. The veil takes on spirit and form through the life we give it in our approach.

Part of the veil's charm, I think, is that it makes us more independent. Even though it appears to be covering the body up and hiding us, in reality, we are free to choose when and how we want to reveal ourselves. It's not a veil we are forced to wear; we are the ones to decide how to play with it, how to express ourselves through it, or how to look for privacy under its wings. The veil takes on spirit and form through the life we give it in our approach.

The veil is feeling; it's perception. It asks us to live in our own bodies and skin. It delicately watches over us and cultivates our mysteries.

…when the piece is danced with creativity and life, the dancers always describe the veil as something more than a casual "accessory."

It's not a veil we are forced to wear; we are the ones to decide how to play with it, how to express ourselves through it, or how to look for privacy under its wings.

The Veil

This is what I'm interested in: when I dance, I search. When I teach the veil dance, I guide the dancers to breathe with it, to feel it on their skin. I ask them to give it time, to follow it, and not to order it around. I invite them to abandon themselves to the ancient language, when the veil was still considered to be a tool of knowledge and it had the role of holy object. Liberally covering yourself up, you can concentrate on the individual, preserve a mystery, increase your mystic introspection.[2] Sometimes we practice a veiled dance without music; we just follow our breathing, which becomes the music, and it's a really sensory experience to be able

The veil can be used with the costumes in many different ways: as a curtain, butterfly wings, a sail, a cape, or a tunic… It's necessary to try different things to find the best way to dance and catch the wind (photo: C. Ferrara).

to dance with calm, deep breaths. We can feel our emotions and our bodies. Every woman is able to find a move that she likes, even if she is picking the veil up for the first time. The veil dance is a creative game; it's not the execution of technical moves that you have to "understand" before carrying out. For a group's first encounter with the veil, I give them a theme or an image to go with, such as "a butterfly in flight," or "a light summer breeze," and I steer clear of giving them technical instruction on how to handle it. You learn more by following the veil with your instinct, even after you already feel comfortable using it.

It's as if it were the movement of the veil itself that suggests new moves for us, which we can find by following it. In this way, we get over the fear of tangling it up or accidentally dropping it on the floor. When it happens that the veil slips from your hands, or gets wrapped around your body, it's not "an error," but a part of the dance's creative game, which doesn't stop, but continues on with what is happening little by little.

The beauty of the symbols is also in their double meanings and ambiguity. In the case of the veil, we draw from the revelation of an elevated wisdom, made possible by removing the veil, as well as covering back up with it. This is a very interesting image for the dance, because it makes it possible to express yourself in depth even when you dance under the cover of the veil in different moves.

The woman has the power to reveal or hide. If she wants, she can discover something in herself as she dances and then express it by covering herself up; by the same token, when she covers herself up, something can be revealed in her dance.

> The veil dance is a creative game; it's not the execution of technical moves that you have to "understand" before carrying out.

The Veil in Ancient Times

I t's very helpful in this type of work to feed the imagination by searching for the veil's meaning in the ancient world, sometimes through our intuition and re-elaboration of the archetypal images, and sometimes through improvisation. There is no detailed information on how exactly the veil was used at that time, because the content of the rituals was kept secret. However, by looking at the veil's symbolism, which refers to psychological not historical matters, its sacred meaning becomes evident and proves that the veil dance's symbol is a ritual instrument from millennia ago.

The word "veil" meant *symbol, sign, spiritual instrument*. In the ancient religions, it was used as a curtain to divide the holy zones from the profane ones, as the meaning of the word itself shows, which comes from the Latin *velum*, meaning curtain. The veil also demonstrated the holiness of precious objects: the statues of divinities were veiled, as were the people who led the spiritual life of the community. The idea of covering with a veil also touches on sexuality and the mystery of conception inside the woman's belly, as we see in the Greek word *hymen*, which was also the name of the deity that personified marriage. The idea of breaking the hymen in the first sexual act is still symbolically referred to when the bride unveils her face to kiss the groom.

The Invisible Dance. The Symbolism of the Veil

191

The Veiled Goddesses

The veil, as a holy and mysterious instrument, belongs instinctively to the Goddesses and was most likely used in the religious rituals dedicated to them, as well as in the later rituals of the Greek worship of Dionysus in the dance of the maenads (bacchae), which were widely depicted in ancient art.

There were many Goddesses connected to this symbolism: the Celtic Goddess Caillech, "the veiled one," had the power of rejuvenation and could turn herself into an old shrew or a beautiful young girl. The veil that she wore seems to have referred to her most mysterious disguise as "fate," the future, and death.[3]

The Greek goddess Harmony wove the veil of the universe, and Aphrodite, who was born from the sea, was assisted by the Seasons who offered her a veil.

The proof of the veil's importance in rituals lies in different myths. For example, in the narrative of the Goddess who descends to the underworld, which was

Dance of the Maenads, 5th century B.C. Capitoline Museums, Rome. (Right).

Bronze figure of a mysterious Greek dancer, 2nd century B.C. Metropolitan Museum. (Left).

The Invisible Dance. The Symbolism of the Veil

The Birth of Venus, marble bass-relief at the Ludovisi throne (470-460 B.C.). Museo Nazione Romano, Rome.

a common myth in many cultures and periods of history. The most well-known version comes from Babylonia, modern day Iraq, and dates back to more than 6500 years ago.

The myth tells of Ishtar's journey to the underworld, when she went to look for her lover Tammuz. During her descent, the Goddess had to pass through seven gates and at each one, she had to give up pieces of her jewelry and clothing until she reached the last gate where she gave up her veil and found Tammuz. This joyous union was celebrated in the spring when the Babylonians gaily danced in praise of nature's rebirth, which was dead and sterile during the absence of the Goddess.

There is another mysterious veil that comes from Egypt, from the worship of Isis who at one time, according to the legend, offered these words:

> *"I am everything that ever was, is, and will be;*
> *and so far, no mortal has ever lifted my veil."*

The image of Isis's veil as the origin, reveals a fluid symbol which, fortunately, cannot be reduced to a simple concept because there are many interpretations. The veil, or the clothing that covered the Goddess's nudity could hide a sacred meaning and the Goddess's warning. The Original Mother, as the mother of all human beings, invites them to keep their distance and have respect.[4]

The veil could represent the spiritual nature of humans. If they want to lift her veil, they have to transcend the limits of individuality and break the boundaries of death, with an immortal soul. It could also be seen as a symbol of the future, and the impossibility of lifting it could represent the curious hesitance of mankind in wanting to know the future: we want to know, but at the same time we are afraid of the revelation of our destinies.

The Invisible Dance. The Symbolism of the Veil

193

Still, the difficulty of lifting Isis's veil could represent mankind's constant effort to see Nature as it really is, in her supreme reality, not veiled by habit or convention.[5]

Of the many possible interpretations of this verse, I like to think that Isis's veil is a symbol of the truth.

She tells us that only through an authentic experience of life can we lift the veil and find a revelation that is both profound and simple: ourselves.

The dance of the Seven Veils and the Goddess's Descent to the Underworld

There is no dance that has a greater air of mystery, mysticism, and feminine resonance than "the dance of the seven veils." It's a dance that has a certain effect on our psyche. Surly Wilde had some idea of this when he had to choose a dance for his Salome and decided on the dance of the seven veils.

In reality, some authors consider the dance of Salome as it is described in the Bible, to date back to the dance of the seven veils that was inspired by the Goddess's descent to the underworld. However, I think this is an unfounded comparison, and one that is hard to support since there are so many contrasting theories on the matter.[6] I prefer to see these as two different dances, because the "dance of the Goddess's descent" was a sensual dance that summoned life through the body, while "Salome's dance" manipulated life, the eroticism of the body, and the veils for a destructive end.

As I said before, the "dance of the seven veils" will probably always remain tied to the dance of Salome, but as a belly dancer myself, I think we should try to rediscover this dance under another light. It should be more closely related to the poetic motivations of the dance of the seven veils, which is a dance of life and transformation, and is the basis of many symbols present in the Goddess's journey of descent in the ancient religions. The original framework of the dance of the seven veils is most likely the descent into the labyrinthine Mother Earth, which was an experience common to many of the archaic Goddesses. The most well-known journeys are Ishtar and Inanna's, which were made so that the Goddesses could truly experience death and rebirth, as well as Astarte's, the

Depiction of the Goddess Demeter, one of the Goddesses of the underworld, who is crying for her daughter Persephone. The story tells us that when Demeter went to look for her daughter, she left the land barren until the Spring, which then became a joyous celebration of her return. Evelyn De Morgan, 1906, London.

Goddess of the Canaanites, Jews, and Phoenicians, who went down to reclaim a lost love.

There are also some variations, for example, Isis who finds Osiris again, not through a descent to the underworld, but through different journeys through swamps and deserted areas, which brings us back to the same mythological theme of descent and rebirth.

In these stories, the theme of completion and fertility is central in the symbols: veils, the underworld, the night, gates, descent, nudity, and the number seven.

The Invisible Dance. The Symbolism of the Veil

195

Sometimes the ancient Egyptians spoke not of the veil of Isis, but the veils or shawls of the Goddess. These were made of seven colors like the rainbow, and she took them when she set off for her trip to the underworld.

On their journeys, the Goddesses had to pass through seven gates (symbol of passage and transformation) and give up a veil at each gate or give up a single veil (which enclosed all of their qualities), in front of the last gate, remaining completely naked.

Like the last phase of the moon, it is here in this seventh region, the kingdom of the dead, the nourishing underground, that the Goddesses remain for three days and three nights, as with the case of Inanna, or for half the year, during the Autumn and Winter, as with the myth of Demeter-Kore, until nature rises again in the Spring.

I think that the veiled dance's essential nature of a sacred dance invites us to cultivate the introspective and instinctive part of us. The veil, in that it's a symbol of the Goddess of Life, is the magical source of every creation and every transformation. The journey to the underworld takes on the meaning of a ritual journey of transformation that we complete through the giving up of our clothes to facilitate a new birth, a spiritual rebirth through the body. The dance of the seven veils celebrates the return to our origins, to the uterus of the earth, where we find secret areas underground that feed our dance and increase our knowledge of ourselves, exemplified in the truth of the naked body.

WORKS CITED IN CHAPTER 3.16

1. T. Bentley, *Sisters of Salomè*.
2. C. Pinkola Estés, *Donne che corrono coi lupi*.
3. B. Walker, *The Woman's Encyclopedia of Myths and Secrets*.
4. J. Campbell, *Mitologia Primitiva*.
5. E. Harding, *I misteri della donna*.
6. W. Buonaventura, *Il Serpente e la Sfinge*, B. Walker, *Encyclopedyia of Myths and Symbols* e A. Mourat, *The Illusive Veil*.

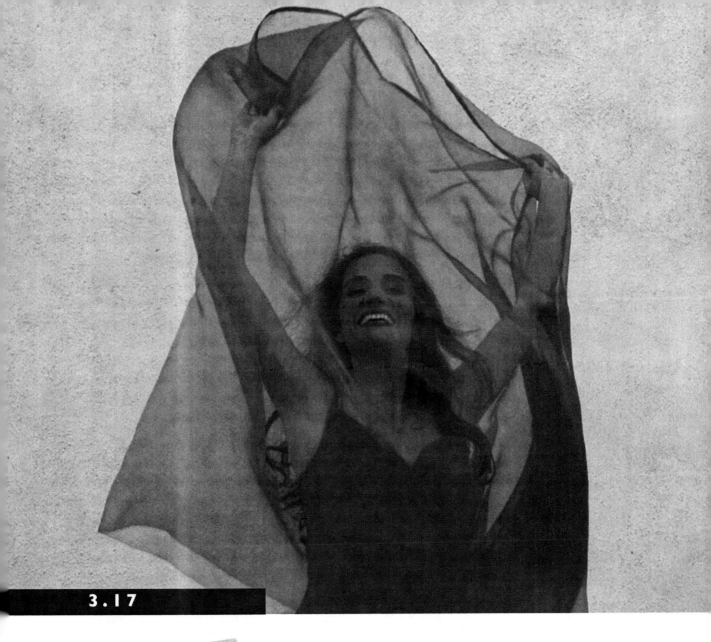

Fire

Fire

It could seem arbitrary to insert the symbol of fire into a feminine context like belly dancing, because usually it is considered to be a more masculine symbol, belonging to the authority of the Father, the supremacy that was brought to life by Apollo in Greek mythology. However, it's precisely because fire and water are opposite elements figuring into the solar and lunar symbolism, that between them there exists a single, harmonious dance. In reality, feeling the presence of this element in belly dancing, confirms for us that it's a very feminine art, one that preserves the dialogue of opposites and truly aims at completeness.

It wouldn't be possible to arrive at the definition of a feminine dance, which we usually consider belly dancing to be, without recognizing the masculine aspect. It would be like defining night without day. I believe that in this dance, which we have defined as a "dance of transformation," there is an implicit idea of the rhythm of opposites, and for this, the symbols of both genders live together in the dance. They alternate, converse, and play. Just as the sun and moon alternate in a day, as we dance, we alternate the elements that feed off of the solar symbolism with the elements of the nocturnal symbolism.

To illustrate this game of opposites more clearly, I'll take the example of the music that we usually use, the type made with the oldest and most essential instruments, the drums and the flute. The music of the *drum*, which excites us with its striking rhythm, and which we interpret with fast, beating movements, is seen as the *masculine aspect*, since it marks the rhythm. Like the sun, it can have variations, but it remains constant. In contrast, the melody of the *flute*, which we interpret with fluid, continuous movements, transforms. It changes like the moon, it unwinds, it comes and goes, it's the *feminine aspect* of the music.

Another beautiful male-female correspondence between these two instruments can be found in the *shape* and *sound* that each has. The flute has a *phallic, masculine shape*, but produces a *feminine melody* with its high-pitched, fluctuating tones. On the other hand, the *drum* has a *dish-like, feminine shape*, but produces a *strong masculine sound*. The musical fusion of these two instruments generates a harmonious union of opposites: in shape, in both masculine and feminine energy, and in the rhythm and melody of the music.

A good part of the dancer's interpretive skill is in her ability to bring out both aspects, at different times during the same varied dance, but also at the same time in two different areas of the body. For example, we might see the rhythm of the drums in her hips and the melody of the flute in her arms.

Like all creative arts, the idea behind the dance is in the game, the exploration of the different possibilities the music has to offer our imagination. Just as in the artistic, harmonious creation, we try to discover both the male and female aspects of the psyche.

In belly dancing's ancient instruments, the drums and the flute, there are opposite elements: the drum has a dish-like, feminine shape and a strong masculine sound, while the flute has a phallic shape and a feminine sound. Woman with a drum, "The Spring," Museum of Napoli, and "Flautist," c. 480 B.C. Tarquinia.

Il sole, simbolo di fertilità

In the language of belly dancing, the symbolism of the sun draws from the continuity of life, regeneration, sexuality, and passion, which are not separated from the spirituality of the body. As a symbol of fertility, the sun (primary symbol of fire) has the ability to give life through its heat and is, more than anything else, the stimulus of periodic regeneration. Significantly enough, in Egyptian hieroglyphics, fire is associated with the idea of life and health.[1] Since it burns and consumes, fire, much like water, is a symbol of purification and regeneration and, as with all the archetypal symbols, it also has a double meaning and importance: the creative aspect that nourishes our human needs with its heat, can also become destructive, cause drought, and reduce us to nothing.

Fire

The dance's fire lives inside us. It's the sexuality that finds a place in the language of our dance, that expresses itself in movements, especially those involving the "forbidden" areas: breasts, hips, pelvis, belly.

Fire's heat is red, which is also the color of life, passion, and blood. The sexual connotations that go along with fire are universally recognized and seem to be connected to the first technique in obtaining it- rubbing to create friction. This is an image of the sexual act and the reproduction of life.[2] For good luck in using the reproductive powers of the sun, different cultures lit fires in front of the door of newlyweds to ensure that they would have many children.[3] The fireplace is also an ancient symbol of fertility that represents the comfort and warmth we find at home, a symbol of the bride and the mother. [4]

Sometimes the procreative aspect of the sun was thought to be the divine feminine source, and was one of the Goddess's gifts, or even her actual body.[5] The idea of belly dancing is associated with the sun in that it is an "Oriental dance." The Orient (oreos) is where the sun is born. In this light, belly dancing is a dance of origin and birth.

The dance's fire lives inside us. It's the sexuality that finds a place in the language of our dance, that expresses itself in movements, especially those involving the "forbidden" areas: breasts, hips, pelvis, belly. It's the passion that we discover inside ourselves and, freeing ourselves from taboo, we are free to express it. It's the spiritual power that, like fire, we can give without consuming ourselves.

WORKS CITED IN CHAPTER 3.17

1. J. Cirlot, *Dizionario dei simboli.*
2. J. Chevalier, A.Gheerbrandt, *Dizionario dei Simboli.*
3. C. Pont-Humbert, *Dizionario dei simboli, dei riti e delle credenze.*
4. A. Stevens, *Il filo di Arianna.*
5. J. Campbell, *Mitologia primitiva.*

CHAPTER 4

Belly Dancing and Sexuality

Now, without taking on the role of sexologist, which doesn't belong to me, I'll try to elaborate on some of the aspects of sexuality that have spontaneously come up in my lessons with groups of women over the years of teaching. Aside from a few innocent jokes about the erotic aspect of belly dancing, usually the women don't talk about their individual relationships with sexuality, probably because they are embarrassed or too modest. In the lessons, I address this subject with humor, respect and straightforwardness, beginning with the instrument of the dance: the body. I don't think that the right teachings of this dance in terms of our sexuality should have to do with complicated erotic positions as in the Kama Sutra (even though the dance does make the hips noticeably looser). I think the secret of sexual knowledge lies in how belly dancing *teaches us to live in our bodies and give to ourselves with love.*

4.1

Is Belly Dancing Provocative?

Usually, the first idea that one has of belly dancing is that it has to do with sexuality in some way, but not so much that of the woman. It seems to emphasize more of an "arousing effect" that provokes the desire of the man watching her.

Usually, the first idea that one has of belly dancing is that it has to do with sexuality in some way, but not so much that of the woman. It seems to emphasize more of an "arousing effect" that provokes the desire of the man watching her. Sometimes we can still hear a dancer presented in this way: "And now, gentlemen, for your pleasure, I present you with our dancer!" This type of show might portray the woman as an object that inspires the longing and attention of others, but doesn't have her own, and doesn't seem to be interested in including other women in her dance.

This stereotype of belly dancing has created a lot of displeasure for me. It has made me turn down job offers. It makes me angry every time I realize how imprisoned belly dancing is in negative models, how much it has lost as an ancient art that honors the female body, and all the feelings that we can experience through it. Over time, it has spurred me to try to do something. To help people get to know this art for what it is, without having to exclude the sexual aspect completely.

It's necessary to clarify the difference between an art that is sensual by nature, like belly dancing, and other shows that would like to be recognized as art and are sometimes interchanged with this dance.

It would be very devaluing to talk about belly dancing as an erotic, "provocative" dance, because a real artist is not vulgar. She doesn't look for a sexual effect with her dance, she doesn't aim at turning her spectators on, or encourage them to act on their desires, turning a fantasy into a physical act. This is the intention of pornography, and I think we should leave it that way.

A real artist is able to get past the conventional image and discover all the aspects that make up the human being and sexuality as a creative energy of life. This is the energy that makes the world go round and has allowed us all to come into existence. This energy that is so important to life is expressed through its dance, belly dancing.

To deny sexuality is to deny Life, but Life itself could never be expressed merely through a provocative dance.

A belly dancing performance can arrive at eliciting desire through a refined eroticism, but if it is real art, the mind of the person watching is raised above that desire. It's doesn't exclude it; it just goes above and beyond.

A belly dancing performance can arrive at eliciting desire through a refined eroticism, but if it is *real art*, the mind of the person watching is *raised above that desire*. It's doesn't exclude it; it just goes above and beyond.

The archaic, cultural aspect of belly dancing recalls a life philosophy that is different from ours, even in regards to sexuality. At that time, the activities concerning the body, such as sexuality and fertility, were holy. There was an infinite series of relationships that weren't limited to the physical outlet, but were interlocked in a complex figuration of life. Gender, sex, and eroticism have the potential to completely transcend the biological sphere. For the ancient religions, sexuality was something infinitely more complex than the one instinctive outlet. It was an authentic workshop where they handcrafted the psychic life.[1] Through it, they sought unity with nature, the melting of tension, and complete relaxation of the being. I'm convinced that belly dancing can still draw from this component that is erotic, but at the same time deliciously sacred. I think this forgotten aspect of the dance, in reality, gives more worth to the woman and gives her the opportunity to experience her body and its spirituality in a new way.

Whoever practices this dance with dedication and is invited to open herself up to its potential, will discover little by little the liberating influence it has on sexual behavior. She will discover that sexuality is not limited to the sexual act or reproduction, because, for as much as it is an act of procreation, our sexuality doesn't exist only within the relationship we have with another person. On the contrary, "it is manifested through the body itself, in the harmonious relationship with life, with other people, with pleasure and with pain, with that which happens around us."[2] It's an experience that begins by having a good relationship with our own bodies.

WORKS CITED IN CHAPTER 4.1

1. G. La Porta, *A come Anima.*
2. E. Chiaia, *Sessualità e crescita personale.*

4.2

The Sensual/Sexual
Aspects of
Belly Dancing

Dancing is the freedom to give through the body and to fill its movements with emotion. But how does belly dancing contribute to liberating the body in a sexual context? Observing the movements of the dance, one thing that becomes obvious is that it is very enjoyable for the person dancing because it follows the desires of the body and doesn't try to "dominate" it or force it into a particular form. In general, the movements are soft and relaxing because they follow a circular cadence and invite us to use our senses- sensual tools- to create the moves, not in a reproduced, mechanical way, but through genuine pleasure. These ample, circular movements, vibration and undulation, naturally belong to the body and, as if in a game, they mix with the libido. During lessons I see the woman who start to take pleasure in this bodily experience, thanks to their discovery of their individual qualities. They are able to let go of their worries about their physical appearance, which can sometimes interfere with desire and make us feel embarrassed, even in a sexual relationship.

To be able to fully enjoy a sexual experience with someone, we need a certain freedom, which starts with our bodies.

Sex is a symbol of unity and perfection. It's a moment of fusion where, ideally, we can relax with our loved one, and where we don't have to worry about the shape of our body. To be able to fully enjoy a sexual experience with someone, we need a certain freedom, which starts with our bodies, and we need to like ourselves enough to be able to share our intimacy with someone else.[1]

The Senses

The senses are the dance's allies because they are the body's gateway to the world. They offer us the possibility to live in it,[2] and therefore, are the tools dancers use to help them get their bodily communication back and to observe and interpret everything that is happening around them. If they say that belly dancing is a sensual dance, it's precisely because in it there is a hidden invitation to discover the purity of the senses and the pleasures that they hold in the body.

Every sense has its turn. We nurture our hearing when we choose our music; touch when we feel the veil on our skin or work with different fabrics; sight with the intentional use of the stare, and also the different colors and styles of the costumes, the choreography, the lights, which can be soft candle light or the strong spotlights of a theater; smell when we use incense and perfumes; but most importantly, we refine the sense of interior hearing when we listen to our deep breathing and improvise however we want.

Sensual/Sexual Aspects of Belly Dancing

Independence

Through the dance we put a game in motion by using our imagination, and starting with the individual, with our bodies. It doesn't passively wait for someone or something to push us from the outside. Many women find great satisfaction in this freedom, in actively defining their own sexuality, in knowing the pleasures and beauty of their bodies. They are asked firsthand- and often for the first time- to invent and to perceive the body with their imagination and senses, and to care about their individual preferences, creating a dance according to the inspiration of the moment.

Only by knowing what it is that really gives us pleasure, can we be free to choose from the many possibilities, both in dancing and our sex lives. Because the discovery of our own creativity helps us get in synch with our partner, it's there that our sexuality can really bloom.[3]

> The dance asks us to perceive the body with the senses and to care about our individual preferences.

Dancing Passion and Love

The love for dancing, which is confirmed in its emotional expression, passion, and feeling, shows us that sexual happiness is not completely separate from love. The love for another human being, or the love for the dance, is a spiritual source. This dance reveals that there is no opposition between carnal love and spiritual love, body and soul, and that both can be found in the same experience.

Sexuality is a medicine for the spirit, and consequently, it is sacred. In fact, Jung observed, and not by chance, that when someone came to his couch complaining about a sexual problem, there real problem was usually with the spirit and the soul more than anything else. On the other hand, a person who spoke about spiritual problems, in most cases really had a problem of the sexual nature.[4]

> Sexuality is a medicine for the spirit, and consequently, it is sacred.

Breathing from the Belly

Another important physical-spiritual component, both in dancing and sex, is breathing freely. When we limit our breathing, the pleasure we get from life, sex, and even dance decreases and creates unwanted tension. As Lowen, the creator of bio-energy affirms, "Holding your breath as the moment of maximum tension gets closer causes the elimination of strong sexual sensations."

Belly dancing helps us establish the right connection between breathing and mobility.

Belly dancing helps us establish the right connection between breathing and mobility, through belly breathing, which is not limited to the upper part of the chest, but manages to include all the way down to the pelvic area. Sometimes I tell my students to think of breathing from the belly button to give them the idea of a deep breath that reaches all parts of the body.

The movements of contraction and relaxation of the belly area create harmony between inhalation and exhalation. It's practically impossible to hold your breath, which would mean not feeling, not expressing our emotions. Through dancing, we learn to breathe with the whole body and not to hold our breath. This is something that can also contribute to a more satisfying physical and emotional sexuality.

An Important Time

For many women, the time dedicated to belly dancing is very special, and they take care of it and protect it like a child: while we dance, we laugh and relax. Usually, if it happens that someone is in a bad mood- because we all have our days- by the end of class she feels lighter, as if the desire to live and keep fighting has come back to her. In this way, we can be more open to life, more relaxed, better able to appreciate the love and affection of the people around us.

A Maternal Tie

Belly dancing has a maternal tie that doesn't create friction between maternity and sexuality. Daughters aren't embarrassed by their mothers when "at their age" they still want to feel their bodies freely through the dance. There's something deep that they discover in it that binds them to it with pleasure and respect.

Abandon

Unblocking the natural mobility of the body, the dance can intensify sexual pleasure, but can also be helpful for women who have a hard time letting themselves go and reaching orgasm during sex. When carrying out the movements of belly dancing, you gain security in abandoning yourself to the sensations of the body. You let go of the idea of having to control the body, because you are invited to let yourself go with the pleasure of the moment. Lowen wrote, "…a total involvement in whatever you are doing is the essential condition of pleasure…the will dissolves and the Ego yields its control to the body. The person who feels pleasure lets her sensations dominate her being."[5]

Through dancing you can learn to experience pleasure, not through the domination of the body, or the rationalization of its movements, or by demonstrating our technical skill and impressive repertoire of steps, but by letting yourself go, abandoning yourself to the movement, instinct, music, sensation, whatever life has to offer at that moment and whatever makes you happy.

Taking things slowly and Experiencing Intimacy

One aspect that is not given much consideration in dancing or sex, is paying attention to the tempo. The dance teaches us that you can choose to follow a constant rhythm- considered to be the masculine aspect of the music- or to follow the melody, which varies greatly- considered to be the feminine aspect. In this way you can vary the tempo, fluctuating between rhythm and melody. Or you can dance in silence, following the rhythm of your breathing, or the beat of your heart. I like the idea that the tempo is a game that can change according to our mood.

Belly dancing and the veil dance carefully cultivate variation and changes in atmosphere. For example, the music can start out with the heavy, upbeat rhythm of percussion, and then continue with the melodic sensual music of a *taksim*. This brings energy into the body, and expresses itself in slow movements or small vibrations that follow the breathing and communicate instinctively with the music, which on the surface seems anarchical and unpredictable.

The dance helps us not to be in a hurry, but to encourage the calmness of its movements. Dancing slowly is one of the most difficult things to do; it frequently requires more courage than dancing to a more lively rhythm. This is not because of the greater technical difficulty in the steps- because a drum solo does demand a lot of talent- but because of the cost it has on the individual; a slow dance is very intimate and it doesn't offer any hiding places. In short, it requires us to reveal ourselves, not to escape that which comes to life inside us. It requires us to take our time, as well. But it's hard to take our time! We're not used to taking our time, especially in front of an audience where it seems like we should "do something" hurry up and show them everything we know how to do. These are motivations that don't help us create, but that can take away the possibility of revealing ourselves.

In the dance, like in love- and I think most people would agree- you shouldn't hurry. Hurrying is the enemy of both artistic creativity and eroticism.

The "joy of taking things slowly" cultivated in belly dancing, can enrich the life of the couple: the desire to "waste a little time," to set aside the "important" obligations and slowly discover yourselves working together in a game.

Through dancing you can learn to experience pleasure, not through the domination of the body, or the rationalization of its movements, but by letting yourself go, abandoning yourself to the movement, instinct...

The dance helps us not to be in a hurry, but to encourage the calmness of its movements.

Feeling like your feet are well-planted on the ground

With the symbol of the land I talked about the importance of staying in contact with the ground when doing the dance's pelvic movements: to feel grounded, with your feet well-planted and your knees slightly bent. This position is indispensable both in the dance and the sexual relationship, because it unblocks the pelvis and allows it to move freely, starting from the ground (even when we're lying down). The application of this idea in the sexual setting can make a big difference in the quality and intensity of the sensations, because with these movements, we actively involve the whole lower part of the body, and not just the genitals. The free movement of the hips increases sensation in the whole pelvic region and makes it easier to let yourself go in wild abandon.[6]

I'd like to point out, however, that not all dances that move the hips give us sexuality and grace: the superficial movements of the hips, which are not "anchored to the ground" can seem sexually exciting, but they deal with a sexuality that is separate from emotion. When the movements are grounded they have a spiritual quality that can be explained by the practices of the ancient religions.[7]

The Lustful Movement of the "Forbidden" Areas

One very evident characteristic of belly dancing is that even though it uses the whole body, it is the "forbidden" areas (breasts, hips, belly) that are most involved. Belly dancing frees us from the damaging chains put on our sexuality. It calls for sexual expression anchored in an animated body that is full of life and that gladly surrenders to the earth, not only in shape or appearance, but in the uninhibited movement of the hips, belly, and breasts. The body doesn't run away from its carnal dimension. With a sensual, sacred gesture, it refutes the conflict between the body and the soul, which is a result of our cultural models.

Belly dancing frees us from the damaging chains put on our sexuality; it calls for sexual expression.

Opening Yourself to Life

T he dance calls us to the height of sensuality, to open our bodies to Life and discover the sacred vision of the female, the sacred origins of existence.

Sexuality calls for a respect for something mysterious that belongs to us, that transcends us, much like what can happen through art that is deeply felt.

From this sacred sexuality the liberating force of the dance gushes forth, and I think its aphrodisiacal-telluric aspect enchants not only the person watching, but also the dancer herself as she abandons herself to its language.

A dancer's poetry, her sensuality, that something that can make an audience dream or cry, lies in the internal gaze she directs at herself while she dances. She summons her body's pleasures and, centering herself on her breathing and belly, expresses the timeless woman that lives inside her. She doesn't need to prove anything to anyone. She's not trying to seduce anyone with her sexy moves. Her dance is something very different from an erotic show; although an erotic show could be beautiful and perfectly executed, it would still be missing the magic and mystery of belly dancing.

Because it is a real art, belly dancing also involves emotion, and through the body it finds the signs that transcend our temporary state. The sacred and the sensual are neighbors living in the psyche and they are "something that for a minute, or forever…change us, shake us, lift us up to the highest point, make our steps dance, allow us to feel an explosion of life."[9]

> Through the dance, the woman reclaims her body; she rediscovers it through the experience of feminine movement, and she lets herself go to the sublime pleasure that, like sexuality, keeps life alive.

Even if a dancer offers her art to those who watch her and creates a dialogue with her audience, she dances for herself, with the divine power that runs through her being. Through the dance, she reclaims her body; she rediscovers it through the experience of feminine movement, and she lets herself go to the sublime pleasure that, like sexuality, keeps life alive.

WORKS CITED IN CHAPTER 4.2

1. P. Young-Eisendrath, *Le donne e il desiderio*.
2. U. Galimberti. *Il corpo*.
3. E. Chiaia, *Sessualità e crescita personale*.
4. C. Pinkola Estés, *Donne che corrono coi lupi*.
5. A. Lowen, *Il piacere*.
6. A. Lowen, *Il piacere*.
7. A. Lowen, *La spiritualità del corpo*.
8. C. Pinkola Estés, *Donne che corrono coi lupi*.

Bibliography

Balaskas, J., *Manuale del parto attivo*, Red, Como, 1990.

Baldacci, M., *Prima della Bibbia. Sulle tracce della religione arcaica del proto-Israele*, Mondadori, Milano, 2001.

Battistini, M., *Dizionari dell'arte. Simboli e allegorie*, Mondadori, Milano, 2003.

Bechtel, G., *Le quattro donne di Dio*, Pratiche, Milano, 2001.

Bentley, T., *Sisters of Salomè*, Yale University Press, New Haven, 2002.

Brooks, G., *Padrone del desiderio*, Sperling & Kupfer, Milano, 1998.

Bonheim, J., *Goddess. A Celebration in Art and Literature*, Stewart Tabori & Chang, New York, 1997.

Buonaventura, W., *Il Serpente e la Sfinge*, Lyra, Milano, 1986.

Campbell, J., *Mitologia primitiva*, Mondadori, Milano, 2004.

Campbell, J., *Il potere del mito*, Tea, Milano, 2000.

Capra, F., *Il punto di svolta*, Feltrinelli, Milano, 1992.

Carlton, D., *Looking for Little Egypt*, IDD Books, Indiana, 2002.

Carotenuto, A., *Jung e la cultura del XX secolo*, Bompiani, Milano, 1998.

Carotenuto, A., *Eros e Pathos. Margini dell'amore e della sofferenza*, Bompiani, Milano, 1997.

Chevalier, J., Gheerbrant, A., *Dizionario dei Simboli*, Rizzoli, Milano, 1999.

Chevel, M., *Il libro delle seduzioni seguito da dieci aforismi sull'amore*, Bollati Boringhieri, Torino, 2001.

Chiaia, E., *Sessualità e crescita personale*, Rizzoli, Milano, 1997.

Cirlot, J., *Dizionario dei simboli*, Milano, Armenia, 2002.

Clottes, J., *La preistoria spiegata ai miei nipoti*, Archinto, Milano, 2002.

Current, R. e Current, M., *Loie Fuller, Goddess of Light*, N. Eastern U. Press, Boston, 1997.

Di Lorenzo, S., *La donna e la sua ombra, Maschile e femminile nella donna di oggi*, Emme, Milano, 1981.

Eliade, M., *La prova del labirinto*, Jaca Book, Milano, 2002.

Eliade, M., *Il sacro e il profano*, Bollati Boringhieri, Torino, 1999.

Eliade, M., *Trattato di storia delle religioni*, Bollati Boringhieri, Torino, 1999.

Galimberti, U., *Il corpo*, Feltrinelli, Milano, 2003.

Gibran, J., *Il profeta*, Rizzoli, Milano, 1993.

Gimbutas, M., *Il linguaggio della Dea*, Neri Pozza, Vicenza, 1997.

Guénon, R., *Simboli della scienza sacra*, Adelphi, Milano, 1984.

Harding, E., *I misteri della donna*, Astrolabio - Ubaldini, Roma, 1973.

Holly, E., *Noble Dreams, Wicked Pleasures. Orientalism in America, 1870-1930*, Princenton University, New Jersey, 2000.

Husain, S., *La Dea*, EDT, Torino, 1999.

Jacq, C., *Il segreto dei geroglifici*, Piemme, Torino, 2001.

Jung, C., *L'uomo e i suoi simboli*, Tea, Milano, 1991.

Lang, A., *Tales from the Arabian Nights*, Wordsworth, Ware, 1993.

Lexova, I., *Ancient Egyptian Dances*, Dover, New York, 2000.

Lowen, A., *La spiritualità del corpo*, Astrolabio, Roma, 1991.

Lowen, A., *Il piacere,* Astrolabio, Roma, 1984.

Lurker, M., *Dizionario dei simboli e delle divinità egizie,* Astrolabio, Roma, 1995.

Mala, M., *Mani magiche,* Armenia, Milano, 1998.

Maraini, D., *La nave per Kobe, diari giapponesi di mia madre,* Rizzoli, Milano, 2001.

Mernissi, F., *L'harem e l'Occidente,* Giunti, Firenze, 2000.

Mernissi, F., *Beyond the Veil,* Schenkman, Massachusetts, 1975.

Monaghan, P., *Le donne nei miti e nelle leggende,* Red, Como, 1987.

Morris, D., *Il nostro corpo,* Mondadori, Milano, 1992.

Mourat, A., *A Comparison of Turkish and Egyptian Oriental Dance,* article, Maryland, 1995.

Mourat, A., *The Illusive Veil,* unpublished manuscript, Maryland, 1995.

Neruda, P., *Odas elementales,* Losada, Buenos Aires, 1991.

Neruda, P., *Residenze sulla terra,* Passigli, Firenze, 1999.

Neumann, *La grande madre,* Astrolabio - Ubaldini, Roma, 1981.

Van Nieuwkerk, K., *A Trade Like Any Other,* University of Texas Press, Texas, 2000.

Nuland, S., *I misteri del corpo,* Mondadori, Milano, 2001.

Pinkola Estés, C., *Donne che corrono coi lupi,* Frassinelli, Milano, 1993.

Pont-Humbert, C., *Dizionario dei simboli, dei riti e delle credenze,* Riuniti, Roma, 1997.

La Porta, G., *A come anima,* Pratiche, Milano, 2001.

Della Portella, I., *Roma sotterranea,* Arsenale, Verona, 2002.

Ravasi, G., *Cantico dei cantici,* Mondadori, Milano, 2004.

Redmond, L., *When the Drummers Were Women. A Spiritual History of Rhythm,* Random House, New York, 1997.

Reik, T., *Psicoanalisi della Bibbia. La creazione della donna, la tentazione,* Garzanti, Milano, 1978.

Rich, A., *Nato di donna,* Garzanti, Milano, 1996.

Risé, C. e Paregger, M., *Donne selvatiche,* Frassinelli, Milano, 2002.

Said, E., *Orientalismo,* Feltrinelli, Milano, 2001.

Serrano, M., *Antigua, vita mia,* Feltrinelli, Milano, 2002.

Sjoo, M., *The Great Cosmic Mother,* Harper-Collins, New York, 1987.

Stevens, A., *Il filo di Arianna. Una guida ai simboli dell'umanità,* Corbaccio, Milano, 2002.

Stewart, I., *Sacred Woman, Sacred Dance,* Inner Traditions Int., Rochester, Vermont, 2000.

Tagore, R., *Gitanjali,* EricArt, Verona, 2003.

Vegetti Finzi, S., *Volere un figlio,* Mondadori, Milano, 1997.

Vercellin, G., *Tra veli e turbanti,* Marsilio, Venezia, 2002.

Voss, J., *La luna nera,* Red, Como, 1996.

Warner, M., *Sola fra le donne. Mito e culto di Maria Vergine,* Sellerio, Palermo, 1980.

Walker, B., *The Woman's Encyclopedia of Myths and Secrets,* Harper-Collins, New York, 1983.

Walker, B., *The Woman's Dictionary of Symbols and Sacred Objects,* Harper-Collins, New York, 1988.

Whitman, W., *Foglie d'erba,* Rizzoli, Milano, 1997.

Young-Eisendrath, P., *Le donne e il desiderio,* Newton & Compton, Roma, 2000.

Bibliography

About the Author

Maria Strova was born in Colombia, where she began studying classical dance at age 12. At 17, she emigrated to the US, where she began studying different styles of modern dance- Graham, Ailey, Cunningham- as well as acting under teachers affiliated with the Actor's Studio. In New York, she worked as a dancer and actress with Ellen Burstyn, Michael Douglas, and Quentin Tarantino.

One day, "by chance," she was walking through the city and discovered belly dancing. From there she set out on the long road of studying and research, which brought her to many different countries to dance and teach. She finally settled down in Italy, where she now lives with her husband and their three children.

She was certified in the study of classical yoga at the Brahmananda school in Rome. She is also interested in the area of maternity in belly dancing, and runs courses on childbirth preparation, incorporating the breathing techniques of yoga as well.

For Maria, belly dancing is a metaphoric, magical means of expression that feeds into the symbolism of the feminine. She considers it to be an art that has a sensual nature and is not unrelated to the sacred experience. It's an artistic form of expression that places value on the woman, the body, instinct, and feminine symbolism. It's an antidote to these violent times we live in.

Her teaching method not only draws from the characteristic language of belly dancing and the veil dance, but it also uses the dance's symbols, acting techniques, and complete breathing. The goal is to eventually know what to do in order to improvise a spontaneous dance, starting at the center of the body.

Maria Strova is the artistic director of the Omphalos Theater (Fiano Romano -Rome), where she holds her Intensive Training Workshops for dancers, as well as the International Dance Festival. For more information, go to *www.danzadelladonna.it.*

TO CONTACT
THE AUTHOR

E-mail:
geadance@libero.it

Address:
MARIA STROVA
Teatro Omphalos – Direzione Artistica
Via Venezia, 35
00065 Fiano Romano (RM)
Italia

For didactic materials on belly dancing (DVD and VHS)
and seminars at the Omphalos Theater:
www.danzadelladonna.it

Index

Scheda bibliografica

Strova, Maria

Il linguaggio segreto della danza del ventre : I simboli, la sensualità, la maternità. Le radici dimenticate / Maria Strova.
Diegaro di Cesena : Macro Edizioni, 2005.

224 p. : ill. ; 27 cm. (Biblioteca del Benessere)

ISBN 88-7507-616-2
CDD 372.13

2679648

Made in the USA